SPECTRUM
MULTIVIEW BOOKS

God & Morality

FOUR VIEWS

EDITED BY R. Keith Loftin

WITH CONTRIBUTIONS BY Evan Fales,
Mark D. Linville, Michael Ruse, Keith E. Yandell

IVP Academic
An imprint of InterVarsity Press
Downers Grove, Illinois

InterVarsity Press
P.O. Box 1400, Downers Grove, IL 60515-1426
World Wide Web: www.ivpress.com
E-mail: email@ivpress.com

*InterVarsity Press® is the book-publishing division of InterVarsity Christian Fellowship/USA®, a movement of
students and faculty active on campus at hundreds of universities, colleges and schools of nursing in the United States
of America, and a member movement of the International Fellowship of Evangelical Students. For information
about local and regional activities, write Public Relations Dept., InterVarsity Christian Fellowship/USA, 6400
Schroeder Rd., P.O. Box 7895, Madison, WI 53707-7895, or visit the IVCF website at <www.intervarsity.org>.*

*Scripture quotations, unless otherwise noted, are from the New Revised Standard Version of the Bible, copyright
1989 by the Division of Christian Education of the National Council of the Churches of Christ in the USA. Used by
permission. All rights reserved.*

*While all stories in this book are true, some names and identifying information in this book have been changed to
protect the privacy of the individuals involved.*

Cover design: Cindy Kiple
Interior design: Beth Hagenberg
Images: ©DNY59/iStockphoto

ISBN 978-0-8308-3984-1

Printed in the United States of America ∞

Library of Congress Cataloging-in-Publication Data

*God & morality: four views / edited by R. Keith Loftin; with
contributions by Evan Fales . . . [et al.].*
  p. cm.
 Includes bibliographical references and index.
 ISBN 978-0-8308-3984-1 (pbk. : alk. paper)
 *1. Christian ethics. 2. Ethics. I. Loftin, R. Keith, 1981- II. Fales,
Evan, 1943- III. Title: God and morality.*
 BJ1251.G57 2012
 171—dc23

   2012027679

P	20	19	18	17	16	15	14	13	12	11	10	9	8	7	6	5	4	3	2	1
Y	29	28	27	26	25	24	23	22	21	20	19	18	17	16	15	14	13	12		

Contents

Introduction

R. Keith Loftin

Questions about morality—how should we act? and why?—have long factored prominently in human thinking. The discussions found in Plato's *Republic* and *Gorgias*, for example, frequently turn on points of morality. Jesus, in his Sermon on the Mount, exhorts his followers to "be perfect . . . as your heavenly Father is perfect" (Mt 5:48). Debates over contemporary social issues, such as abortion and embryonic stem cell research, regularly take shape in moral terms, and we teach our children to conduct themselves morally.

Various more or less successful ethical systems have been proposed for assessing moral issues.[1] These systems typically articulate notions of right and wrong that guide conduct and provide a framework for analyzing ethical dilemmas. That is, in general terms, the task of ethics proper. Antecedent to ethics proper, however, are questions regarding the source and nature of ethical concepts. This is the province of metaethics: a sort of philosophizing about ethics proper. This book brings together two atheist and two Christian theist philosophers to present the four main positions on the central metaethical questions: Where does morality come from? What, if any, is God's role vis-à-vis morality? Is God necessary for morality? Are morals objective or relative? How do we come to know moral truths?

History has seen a wide variety of responses to these questions.

---

[1]See Scott B. Rae, *Moral Choices: An Introduction to Ethics*, 3rd ed. (Grand Rapids: Zondervan, 2009) for a helpful presentation of such systems.

Many have thought the connection between God and morality so strong as to support an argument for God's existence. Indeed, throughout the nineteenth and into the twentieth century such moral arguments were standard fare among natural theologians (where natural theology is the project of bolstering the case for theism apart from any special divine revelation). After waning in popularity during the Enlightenment, moral arguments for God's existence are enjoying renewed interest today.

A common misunderstanding in the debate over the connection, if any, between God and morality stems from the mistaken conflation of two distinct questions: Is God necessary for morality? and, Can a person lead a morally praiseworthy life without believing in God? The former, an inquiry into the metaphysical foundation or grounding of morality, is an important metaethical issue. The latter is an epistemological inquiry, wholly apart from the metaethical question of morality's foundation. This misunderstanding has been perpetuated by John Locke, for example, who confusedly claimed: "Those are not at all to be tolerated who deny the Being of a God. Promises, Covenants, and Oaths, which are the bonds of Humane Society, can have no hold upon an Atheist. The taking away of God, tho but even in thought, dissolves all."[2] Contrary to Locke, the philosopher who perceives a strong connection between God and morality may happily grant the non-theist's ability to lead a morally praiseworthy life. She will nevertheless insist that the non-theist's foundation for morality is insufficient.

Undoubtedly the most persistent objection to beset theistic accounts of morality is the Euthyphro dilemma. Tracing back to Plato's *Euthyphro*, the objection asks whether something is good because God approves of it, or if God approves of something because it is good. The first horn of the dilemma is an attempt to inveigle the theist into admitting that the good is arbitrary because God might just as well have approved hatred and malice. In that case hatred and malice would be good, which seems decidedly implausible. The second horn is an attempt to lure the theist into admitting that the foundation or basis of

---

[2]John Locke, *A Letter Concerning Toleration*, ed. James Tully (Indianapolis: Hackett, 1983), p. 51.

morality lies beyond or exists independently of God, which seems to undercut the perceived dependence of morality upon God.

Thus far I have used the term *moral(ity)* rather loosely, and the reader will presently discover that the term is used in conflicting ways. More specifically, there is a fundamental disagreement about the nature of moral principles. On the one hand, moral realists conceive of moral principles as objective—that is to say, moral principles are universally valid for all people at all times (regardless of what anyone happens to think). Moral nonrealists, on the other hand, generally conceive of moral principles as relative (or subjective)—that is to say, instead of being objective, moral principles are dependent upon circumstances or what people think.[3] Two additional terms need mentioning. The term *naturalism,* for present purposes, may be defined as the denial of the existence of God coupled with the belief that all of reality (including morality) is ultimately explainable in terms of natural facts. Opposed to naturalism is *theism,* which we may define simply as belief in God's existence. Having thus whet your appetite for the discussion that follows, let us turn to the main essays.

Michael Ruse is the Lucycle T. Werkmeister Professor of Philosophy at Florida State University, where he also directs the Program in History and Philosophy of Science. An ardent proponent of Darwinian naturalism, Ruse has published numerous books and articles, including *Taking Darwin Seriously* (Prometheus Books, 1998) and *Biology and the Foundation of Ethics* (coedited with Jane Maienschein, Cambridge University Press, 1999). In his chapter, "Naturalist Moral Nonrealism," Ruse defends the view that morality is, like all the rest of reality, entirely the result of naturalistic evolution. God plays no role in morality because God does not exist. Arguing strenuously that our common perception of morality as objective is illusory, Ruse maintains that our various moral principles exist but only as psychological beliefs useful for our flourishing; morality has no transcendental grounding.

Evan Fales is associate professor of philosophy at the University of Iowa, where he has taught for thirty-seven years. Fales's extensive pub-

---

[3]I say "generally" because those who deny the existence of moral principles altogether are also called moral nonrealists.

lications in the philosophy of religion, epistemology and metaphysics include *Causation and Universals* (Routledge, 1990), *A Defense of the Given* (Rowman and Littlefield, 1996), and *Divine Intervention: Metaphysical and Epistemological Puzzles* (Routledge, 2009). Though he agrees with Ruse that God plays no role in morality because God does not exist, Fales argues in "Naturalist Moral Realism" that moral principles are objective in nature. These moral principles, he argues, are grounded in certain facts about human persons that have resulted from purely natural evolutionary processes.

Keith Yandell is the Julius R. Weinberg Professor of Philosophy at the University of Wisconsin-Madison. He has written *Hume's "Inexplicable Mystery": His Views on Religion* (Allyn and Bacon, 1971), *The Epistemology of Religious Experience* (Cambridge University Press, 1993), and *Philosophy of Religion* (Routledge, 1999), as well as numerous papers on God and morality. He argues, in "Moral Essentialism," that though God does exist the truth of moral principles does not depend upon him. This is because moral principles, if true, are necessary truths—truths that exist as either abstract objects or the propositional content of divine thoughts. Yandell's position is similar to that of Fales in interesting ways, though Yandell does preserve for God the role of moral exemplar for humans: God may be seen as the model of moral flourishing whom humans strive to resemble.

Mark Linville teaches philosophy at Clayton State University. In addition to numerous articles and book chapters, including "The Moral Argument" in *The Blackwell Companion to Natural Theology* (Wiley-Blackwell, 2009), Linville is the coeditor (with David Werther) of *Philosophy and the Christian Worldview* (Continuum, 2012) and is the coauthor (with Paul Copan) of *The Moral Argument* (Continuum, forthcoming). In "Moral Particularism" Linville argues that moral principles are objective in nature and ultimately dependent upon God. Distinguishing his view from classical divine command theory, according to which God's commands are constitutive of morality, Linville argues it is God's nature that is the standard for morality. Our moral obligations toward one another, then, arise from our being created in the divine image.

Each contributor offers an essay explicating his view of God and morality. Each of these main essays is followed by a brief response from each other author, allowing the reader to benefit from their dialogue. The result is, I think, an excellent starting place for investigating the central metaethical questions.

The contributors—Evan Fales, Michael Ruse, Keith Yandell and Mark Linville—have my appreciation for their hard work and patience. It has been my pleasure to work with each of them. I am grateful also to Gary Deddo, our editor at InterVarsity Press, for his support. Finally, I am thankful to my father-in-law, Dr. Gary Greene, who passed away during the course of this project, for his abiding example of Christlikeness. It is to him that I dedicate this book.

1

Naturalist Moral Realism

Evan Fales

YOU AND I HAVE OUR DIFFERENCES: you have your personality, ambitions and idiosyncrasies; I have mine. We also share something important: a common human nature. That nature, so I will argue, provides the basis for morality. The moral norms in question are perfectly objective—just as human nature is an objective feature of our existence. These norms are norms for human behavior. If human nature were different in certain ways, the norms would be different, and they might differ for intelligent species (if there are any in the universe) whose natures differ importantly from our own. If, for example, such creatures reproduced sexually, but matings required three participants, their sexual morality would diverge interestingly from ours. But this in no way offers support for moral relativism or nihilism. It just means that what is right and good is so always *for* beings of a certain kind. So I shall argue.

An adequate defense of naturalist moral realism (NMR) must accomplish at least the following things:

1. provide an *analysis* of objective moral truth

2. provide an ontological *grounding* for such truths

3. provide a basis for various ethical distinctions (e.g., the distinction between the morally obligatory and the supererogatory)

4. explain how moral truths are knowable by us

5. show how such truths can be squared with our moral intuitions

I cannot accomplish all of these tasks here in detail, but I hope to sketch the view in sufficient detail to make it plausible.

DEFINING NMR

The two distinguishing features of NMR require a bit of elucidation. Both *naturalism* and *realism* are contested terms.[1] For present purposes I will take naturalism to involve, minimally, a commitment to there being no disembodied minds. More robustly, we may take a naturalistic ethics to be an ethical theory that seeks to understand the content and origins of human moral norms in terms of the age-old wisdom of folk psychology and, at least in some difficult cases, in terms of a scientific understanding—which will minimally include psychology, primate ethology, paleoanthropology and neo-Darwinian models—of the origins and nature of *Homo sapiens*.[2]

Moral realism is the view, roughly, that moral norms are not simply "made up" by people: their existence isn't a matter of what someone or some group thinks they are. Of course, moral norms must be sensitive to human mental states, because such states are an essential component of human nature. But that doesn't mean that moral norms are dictated by what people take to be right and wrong. Rather, they are determined by the facts—by certain facts about persons (and other creatures), in particular.

---

[1]For different uses of *naturalism* see Evan Fales, "Naturalism and Physicalism," in *The Cambridge Companion to Atheism*, ed. Michael Martin (New York: Cambridge University Press, 2006), pp. 118-34. My use of the term *natural* is meant to contrast with *supernatural*.

[2]There are thorny issues in this neighborhood, in particular respecting whether moral properties (and normative properties generally) are, or can be reduced to, natural properties. It does not help that there is no clear criterion by which to distinguish natural properties from those that are not. A common suggestion is that they are the properties recognized by physics or the ones that a "final physics" would recognize. That is, if not question begging, at least unhelpful. By those lights, the property of being alive may well not be a natural property (it being doubtful that it is reducible to properties recognized by physics)—to say nothing of mental properties. But by my lights, these are all natural properties. My aim here at any rate is to exclude properties that must be grounded in a supernatural being. I take naturalism, minimally, to be committed only to the claim that there are no disembodied minds. Here, however, a stronger claim can be adopted: let the admissible entities and properties be just those whose existence has a neo-Darwinian explanation. That will exclude divinely grounded and revealed moral truths, and, for example, divinely infused human souls.

This does not entail, however, there being no place within morality for human decisions and conventions. There are at least two ways that these can play a significant role. First, they may govern the ways in which certain morally charged attitudes and intentions may be expressed or conveyed to others. Second, conventions may reasonably be instituted to settle certain sorts of moral dilemmas.

Take politeness, which is a form of kindness. Its exercise is, if not always imperative, at least a significant characteristic of morally sensitive behavior. There are certain behaviors that are intrinsically impolite: rudeness in the form of gratuitous insult, for instance. Other behaviors—bringing a gift one knows will be enjoyed in responding to a dinner invitation—are by nature exercises in politeness. But much that counts as polite behavior is culture bound and conventional: its very stereotypy plays an essential role in successfully signaling the intention to respect and appreciate others. So moral requirements on behavior can quite properly be arbitrary in this limited way.

How can convention properly play a role in the settling of moral dilemmas? Let's once more consider politeness. Politeness and honesty are values that often clash in their application. Being socially insecure, I ask your opinion about whether I'm handsome. Fact is, you find me ugly as a pug. When should tact trump candor? One can easily imagine scope for cultural norms or conventions to (more or less) settle such matters. But the question of objective justification nevertheless remains always in play.

With these qualifications understood, we can take the project of defending NMR to be the task of showing how facts about human nature (and about other beings that have moral standing) determine objective truths about what one should and should not (and may and may not) do.[3]

---

[3]One important contrast between my position and certain other metaethical views concerns a different understanding of the exercise of free will and its relation to moral autonomy. On my view, the exercise of free will *just is* the making of choices by way of rational deliberation and then acting because a given action alternative has thereby come to be understood to be as good as or preferable to any other. This account satisfies the constraints upon a libertarian conception of freedom inasmuch as it accords with the requirement that an agent have *control* over his or her free actions, while also denying that the process of choice—the execution of a practical syllogism—is (though natural) a *causal* process: hence causal determination is eschewed, and the problem of ancestral determination is escaped. For details on this account, see Evan Fales,

But what are these facts, and how do they determine the truths in question?

THE ONTOLOGICAL GROUND OF MORAL TRUTHS

The moral metatheory I'm going to sketch grounds truths about moral permission and obligation on truths about what is good or bad, and takes goodness and badness always to be goodness or badness *for* a certain being or type of being. But what sorts of facts about a being, describable in a non-question-begging naturalistic way, are those in terms of which those good or bad things are to have their goodness or badness understood?

The starting point for an answer to this question involves appeal to the notion of a teleologically organized system (TOS). A TOS is an entity organized so as to have some (or possibly more than one) end, goal or purpose. We may distinguish those TOSs whose *teloi* are imputed from those whose *teloi* are intrinsic or original (ITOSs). So, for example, a can opener has the purpose it does because it was designed for that purpose or is, at least ordinarily, used for that purpose. (If I am stranded on a desert island with lots of canned goods but no manufactured can opener, I might press a sharp rock into service to serve that end; by imputation, it has now become my can opener, even though it's a found object.) But original teleology is not something conferred on an entity by some other being, some being whose intentions and purposes it serves. My intentions vis-á-vis any mosquito in my vicinity are mostly lethal, but the mosquito has its own "intentions"—even if not conscious

---

"Is Middle Knowledge Possible? Almost," in *Sophia* 50 (2011): 1-9. However, I insist that, ultimately and in general, what *count* as reasons that properly inform practical deliberation are known facts about our circumstances and nature that themselves are not chosen and that typically have causal etiologies. In this, the view contrasts with libertarian views on which the locus of freedom lies in the exercise of choice over which sorts of things we will count *as reasons for us* in a given choice situation (and which regard the deliberative process that proceeds from those reasons to be a causal one).

The basic problem for all such views is that they leave it a mystery how, in the end, choice is to be *justified*, for there is no *further* appeal to reasons to be had (on pain of regress) to justify the choice of certain ultimate reasons as relevant. If, ultimately, *reasons* can't be offered in justification for our choice of ends—reasons grounded in our motivations, circumstances and natures and those of the fellow beings affected by our actions—then I fail to see how the choice of ends can be anything other than arbitrary, and hence lethal to morality.

ones. Some ends can subserve others: (female) mosquitoes are by nature bloodsuckers. That end subserves the end of procreation. Other ends are final ends; for almost all biological organisms these include health and procreation (and, for human beings, they include happiness and knowledge). Some ends may be both final and means to other ends.

Can teleological properties be analyzed in terms of or reduced to nonteleological ones? I'm not going to enter that debate here. But I am going to insist that intrinsic teleological properties are to be found in the natural world: there are *natural* ITOSs. Nor must an ITOS be conscious: intrinsic teleology can be found in systems that do not possess consciousness. An acorn's *telos* is to grow into an oak. An oak tree's *teloi* are to flourish (in an oakish sort of way) and to produce more acorns. It is as plain, and open to empirical inspection, whether an oak achieves these ends or whether it does not—and that it *has* these ends—as are the tree's branches or its height. These are all equally *natural* features of the oak.

The natural ends of an oak are connected, obviously enough, with the things that are *good for* and *bad for* it. Flourishing, for example, *just is* an oak-tree good. Other things—adequate water and sunlight—are good for oak trees because they are means to (causally necessary for) intrinsic oak-tree goods. So, roughly, we may say that the intrinsic goods for an ITOS are the states of affairs that constitute achievement of its ultimate ends, and the instrumental goods are those that serve or promote those ends.[4]

Although I have not attempted to offer a reductive account of teleological organization in terms of the nonteleological physical features and/or causal history of ITOSs (and hence no such account of their purposes or ends), I do claim that there are such beings, and that their existence and teleological properties are open to empirical inspection. Moreover, I take it to be not seriously deniable that such beings—including conscious beings, many of whose ends are reflected

---

[4]Might there not be intrinsic goods and evils that are not good or bad *for* any being as such, but simply good or bad *simpliciter*—things or states of affairs that are such that, as it were, it is simply a good or bad thing absolutely that the universe contain them? Perhaps it's good that the universe contain beings of a certain sort—intelligent beings, for example, or social beings. But I'll not pursue this matter here.

in or determined by conscious purposes and intentions—arose by way of natural evolutionary processes. It has, however, been denied: indeed often denied by theists. (They don't deny that there are such beings, of course, but they deny that they could have arisen by purely naturalistic processes.)

Now theists who question the adequacy of naturalistic explanations of purpose have put their fingers on a significant lacuna in naturalistic accounts of the world. I think that at the heart of the explanatory gap upon which theists are pressing is the problem of original intentionality. Conscious purposes require intentions: it is precisely a distinctive feature of intentional states that they can be directed toward nonexistent objects, and future-directed purposes typically envision precisely such objects or states of affairs. What's worse, the problem of accounting for original intentionality is, I believe, the really *hard* problem of consciousness. So here the naturalist is, admittedly, caught flat-footed.

Are theists any better off? Many certainly think so. Christian theists hold that God made us in his image,[5] a core aspect of which is to possess the accoutrements of personhood: conscious awareness, intentional states, reason, purposes and a will. But theists *do not tell us how God manages to do this*. There's a problem here, just as for the Darwinian naturalist. Beings with intrinsic intentions and purposes can confer purposes "by imputation" to systems designed with a relevant teleological organization. We design computers to perform astonishing feats of reasoning. But that's a derived intentionality. Computers lack original intentionality; how could anyone manufacture a computer, however ingeniously, whose physical coding of information constituted *intrinsically* intentional states with *intrinsic* reference—that is, original intentionality?

Very well: but then, how does *God* manage it? Is he just *smarter* than we are? He takes some dirt, maybe mixes in a bit of divine spittle and shapes the clay into an "image" (*tselem*) of himself, breathing into it some divine "breath" (*ruach*). *That* can't be the story: it explains nothing. All right: God takes some organic matter and fashions a human

---

[5]At least *male* human beings (see 1 Cor 11:7).

body with all the organs and cellular structures that human bodies have. And then what? How is this not just a divine artifact with (at best) imputed intentionality? But theists say that's not the end of the story: *and then* God adds a rational soul. If this is supposed to be an explanation, we need to hear more. *A great deal* more: what sort of thing is a soul, and how does God create one—in particular, how does he give it original intentionality and purpose? How is creation of beings that possess original intentionality possible? Clearly it can be done somehow: here we are. But until we understand *how* it can be done, we've no basis for claiming that God can do it, but nature cannot.

A moral theory must specify not only the ontology of the good and the bad, but also the ontology of the right and the wrong. It must distinguish the morally obligatory from the permissible and the forbidden, and must distinguish also the morally neutral permissibles from those that are good, and hence which are, if not obligatory, supererogatory.[6] Our guiding principle is this: those things that are good are the things for which one ought to strive. Of course this is hopelessly underspecified as it stands. Let's begin to qualify it. First, we must limit "oughts" to "achievables." Some goods may be beyond our reach. Second, something's being good provides a reason for bringing it into existence. But a reason for whom? For those the state of affairs benefits? Or also for others? Third, "oughts" are *prima facie* obligations. The moral life is pervaded by moral dilemmas. Faced with competing "oughts," we must grapple with the task of determining and doing what's best under our circumstances. But these are problems for every moral theory.

More pressing for the naturalist are these questions: Committed to striving for the good, for *whose* goods ought we to strive, and why? How shall we distinguish things that are merely good to strive for from those we are under an obligation toward? And does the obliga-

---

[6]Robert Adams claims that divine commands serve to distinguish the morally obligatory from the merely supererogatory (Adams, *Finite and Infinite Goods: A Framework for Ethics* [Oxford: Oxford University Press, 1999], pp. 260-61). Obviously, the naturalist can't avail him- or herself of this explanation. Nor should he or she want to: either God's way of making the division is well motivated or else it's morally *arbitrary*. If it's the former, then the naturalist can avail him- or herself of the same justifying reasons that prompt God's decisions about what to command and what to leave to human benevolence.

tion to strive for the good commit one to a narrowly consequentialist ethical theory?

We may approach the first question by noting that morality concerns primarily questions about how we ought to treat other human beings. That's no accident: we are, in a very fundamental way, a social species. Social relationships with other human beings are not merely instrumentally useful to us but lie at the very core of our personhood, and thus rank high among ends that are ultimate for us.[7] So among the "oughts" most central to our existence are those that promote social flourishing. (We may speak also of obligations we have to ourselves, but, if only as a terminological matter, we think of the sphere of morality as the sphere of other-regarding obligations. Perhaps—see later—these are not as distinct as they may seem.) However, we also have moral obligations toward humans and other creatures with whom we share no (direct) social relationships. I suggest a naturalist account of those obligations later.

Every moral theory faces the question, Why be moral? Ethical egoism provides a ready answer: do just what serves my self-interest; goals that benefit me are inherently reason-giving for me, and those that don't aren't. For the ethical naturalist who rejects egoism, the question is especially pressing: evolutionary theory suggests that the primary unit of selection is the individual, and one ought therefore to expect that an individual's *telos* includes, above all, self-preservation (and successful procreation).[8] It's an open question, however, how we came by the natures we possess and the ends those natures determine.

In my view, the ethical naturalist ought to respond to the question Why be moral? in very much the same vein as Plato and Aristotle. However acquired, we have a soul (in the ancient Greek sense), so or-

---

[7]Quite grisly experiments by Harry Harlow in the 1950s demonstrated the dramatic and permanent effects of social deprivation on infant monkeys. They became psychological basket cases; but the data revolutionized infant-care practices in this country. Data from feral children and children raised under conditions of extreme social deprivation amply confirm Harlow's findings. See Kendra Cherry, "The Science of Love: Harry Harlow and the Nature of Affection," *About.com*, http://psychology.about.com/od/historyofpsychology/p/harlow_love.htm.

[8]There is a lively debate over the role of group selection by way of Darwinian processes. Group selection would provide a biological basis for the ascription of social *teloi* that constitute reasons for group members to act in ways that benefit group welfare.

dered that virtue is its own reward—more precisely, it provides the greatest rewards a soul can enjoy. Conversely, vice breeds the greatest harms the human soul can suffer. Theists will perhaps not disagree; they'll disagree with me about how we got such a soul, and they'll disagree about whether the rewards and harms are scheduled for this life only. Defending the claim itself is not something I'll undertake here; nor can I hope to do better than Plato and Aristotle themselves.[9]

Is the theory a consequentialist one? Is rightness or wrongness a function of the goods and harms produced (or likely produced) by a given action? Not necessarily—not, at least, if goods and evils are evaluated by summing utilities in the manner of classical utilitarian theories. For example, we ought to consider distributive justice an end of the highest importance, for the demand for fairness is as deeply imbedded a feature of our social natures as any.[10] More generally, moral imperatives are to be determined by the basic features of human nature, especially as it is oriented toward relationships with others and community well-being, and not in terms of some narrowly conceived notions such as pleasure and pain.[11]

---

[9]See Plato, *Meno* and *The Republic*, and Aristotle *Nicomachean Ethics*. More recently, a similar view has been defended by Philippa Foot in her *Natural Goodness* (Oxford: Clarendon Press, 2001); I am largely in agreement with her views. There is a significant critical literature, which I cannot properly address here, but see footnote 11.

[10]It appears also to be one of the most primitive, if not the most primitive, of moral instincts. This is true both developmentally, for infants, and evolutionarily; many monkey species and apes understand when they have been cheated. It is less clear whether apes are ever capable of recognizing, and resenting, unfairness to others, as humans are (see Frans de Waal, *Primates and Philosophers: How Morality Evolved*, ed. Stephen Macedo and Josiah Ober [Princeton, N.J.: Princeton University Press, 2006], pp. 44-49). For a recent study of the neurological basis of the sense of fairness in humans, see E. Tricomi, A. Rangel, C. F. Camerer and J. P. O'Doherty, "Neural Evidence for Inequality-averse Social Preferences," *Nature* 463 (2010): 1089-91.

[11]Although many of the *teloi* of organisms are plainly evident, the issue is contentious, especially in certain sorts of cases, raising the question of what the bases are for teleological properties. Consider the fact that different "levels" of teleology can be ascribed to the same item. So for artifacts: a credit card may be a more or less versatile instrument of monetary exchange *and* a more or less versatile break-in device in a robber's tool kit.

The natural ends of organisms, their flourishing, their natural role in defending a community of con-specifics or alter-specifics (as in symbiosis and certain forms of altruism), and their role in passing on a certain complement of genes to the next generation: are these compatible ends? Is one primary? Are they connected? William FitzPatrick, for example, attacks Foot's "welfare-based" teleology on the grounds that (1) teleological organization is a function of how the parts of a system came to be assembled so as to work together nonaccidentally, and (2) that the working of organisms is most fundamentally directed toward promoting gene propagation, which can

But which goods trigger moral obligations? And which remain optional? The first feature of the distinction between the obligatory and
supererogatory that requires attention is that there's no sharp line of de-
marcation (a fact not easy for the divine command theorist to account for).
A truer reflection of our moral lives recognizes a range of cases, from clear

---

conflict with individual welfare (*Teleology and the Norms of Nature* [New York: Garland, 2000]).

Take worker honeybees, whose defense of the hive is a suicide mission. Worker bees are
functioning properly, but not on behalf of their own welfare, when they attack an intruder. In
Foot's defense, one might reply in two ways: (1) Being programmed to sting intruders is something that works for Maya the bee's welfare (as long as all her sisters and sisters of her ancestors
are/were similarly programmed), for even though use of her stinger is fatal, failure to have the
program (which ordinarily could not happen unless her tribe lacked stingers) would be even
more damaging, on average, for her prospects for flourishing, given the bee way of life. (2) One
could concede FitzPatrick's point, but insist that Maya exhibits also a level of teleology not
reducible to the aim of gene propagation and relative to which defensive proclivities are indeed
a threat. After all, there are conditions organisms can undergo that, whatever their *instrumental*
value for the propagation of genes, are *intrinsically* good or evil: pleasure and pain, for example,
and the acquisition of knowledge for innately curious human beings. These are goods or harms
to which, *qua* intrinsic value, the aim of gene propagation is blind.

Maya offers one sort of case; here's another: it has been suggested—let's assume correctly—
that Irish elk went extinct because sexual selection for antler size drove antler dimensions to
the point where male elk could no longer navigate through dense Irish forests. Pity the elk: here
the very forces that drive organisms toward effectiveness as gene propagators drove Bullelk and
his ilk into a cul-de-sac. He was saddled with a nature, *qua* gene propagator, that harbored two
sub-*teloi* locked in mortal combat with one another; his evolutionary "choices" were to remain
celibate or immobile. In order to flourish as a gene propagator, Bullelk needed to have huge
horns—and to lack them. Such is the stuff of tragedy. Nevertheless we can say all manner of
things about what sort of life would have constituted flourishing for Bullelk: plenty of food and
water and mates, absence of disease and pain, and so on.

FitzPatrick disallows that an organism can realize such distinct natural teleological structures (ibid., pp. 116-17). He imagines, e.g., a machine designed by a scientist that is so sophisticated that it makes sense to speak of the machine's *welfare*. The designer, nevertheless,
has no interest in its welfare, but designs with the sole intention of promoting propagation of
certain features called *schmenes*. FitzPatrick would have us concede that welfare considerations
have nothing to do with the teleology of the machine. My appraisal of the case is diametrically
opposed to his: clearly the welfare of the machine constitutes a *good* for it—one good for it, if
possible, to pursue. I go further: if the machine is capable of experiencing *pain* and *pleasure*,
then its designer has a *moral obligation* not wantonly to subject it to the former, no matter his
actual intentions in designing the machine. Were I asked: Why do pleasure and absence of pain
constitute intrinsic *ends* for such a machine, I should not know how to reply, except to say to my
interrogator, "Have *you* ever experienced pain?"

Abjuring a full-dress response to FitzPatrick, I must comment that his positive metaethical
view, which appeals to our faculty of reason and our ability to arrive at a "*reasoned conception of the
good*, rather than being led about primarily by appetites and instincts directed ultimately at maxi-
mizing . . . replication of our genes" is an account with a gaping hole. What *are* the reasons that
ground such a conception of the good, and if not grounded in human nature, then how can they
fail to be either arbitrary or conventional? In fact FitzPatrick's extremely sketchy remarks suggest
a quite ordinary appeal to facts about pain and pleasure, desires and the like (ibid., pp. 367-69) that
because he takes them to involve natural faculties, make his ethics as robustly naturalistic as mine.

obligation to pure supererogation. Between lies a vast terrain where the best assessment is that obligation comes in degrees. If—heaven forefend— my thirty-year-old son is arrested, do I have a moral obligation to provide his bail? If a good friend loses her shirt at poker, am I morally obligated to stand her a loan? There is no way to decide such cases without further fleshing out, but many such elaborations will generate a weak obligation.

That said, I offer the following suggestion: moral obligations derive from those ends, general pursuit and achievement of which is (vaguely enough) essential to the well-being of creatures that qualify as having moral standing. Moral obligation is also agent sensitive: a moral obligation often depends on the nature of one's relationship to those affected by an action—that is, whether one has assumed contractual or other responsibilities toward them.

THE KNOWABILITY OF MORAL FACTS

It should be evident from what has been said about the ontology of moral facts how they can come to be known. Some moral imperatives are obvious: do not murder, steal or lie (other things being equal). Others are far from obvious, either because the morally relevant circumstances are hard to know or very complex, or because we're faced with a difficult moral dilemma. Some have held that moral truths are *necessary* truths, knowable a priori. Others deny that there are (objective) moral truths at all. The naturalist should hold, say I, that some moral truths are empirically knowable, others a priori.

What I mean is this: there are *conditional* moral truths of the form:

* If a being S of type X interacts with a being T of type Y in circumstances C, then S ought/ought not to perform an action of type A.

(Here X and Y are descriptions that include or entail the teleological facts about S and T.) Such truths are *conceptual* truths that are, in principle, knowable a priori. But knowledge that S and T are teleologically organized as they are is an empirical matter, and so

** S ought/ought not to act toward T by performing action A in circumstances C

is a truth that can only be known by empirical investigation. It is, in

particular, an empirical question how human beings ought to treat one
another, one that can be ascertained only through knowledge of how
we're teleologically ordered. Some truths about our teleological organization are obvious, yielding obvious moral truths; others are not and
may even require sustained scientific investigation.

But what about the role of moral intuitions? There's no denying that
moral intuitions play an essential role in our practical lives. The question, however, is whether (some) moral truths can be *known* simply by
way of intuition. Moral intuitionists have thought so, but I am skeptical. What sort of a thing is a moral intuition? If it's simply a strong
conviction, derived not from an explicit chain of reasoning but in some
way that subjectively appears more "direct," that is not incompatible
with its having been arrived at actually by way of a complex history of
experiences and tacit inferences, the details having been forgotten or
perhaps never subject to explicit attention. Intuitions of that sort might
qualify as knowledge generating.

But moral intuitions are often thought of as moral *instincts:* capacities
for judgment (and feeling) that are inborn, not born of experience. They
may have sensory *triggers*, but they don't involve reasoning from empirical premises to moral truths. Such intuitions may well count as providing moral knowledge on a reliabilist epistemology. They'd do so, provided, for example, that they're cognitive faculties hard-wired into
(normal) human psyches as a result of evolutionary processes that reli-
ably selected for instincts responsive in the right way to human needs
and goods. But as I'm no reliabilist, I'd deny that this sort of selective
history—which is not unlikely—confers upon judgments so derived the
status of knowledge. Moral instincts selected for in this way may nevertheless be extremely reliable *indicators* of (prima facie) moral duties.

It will be apparent from what I've said about both the ontology and
the epistemology of moral truths that I'm no friend of Hume's is-ought
distinction. I'd be happy enough to agree that there's no *formal* entailment relation between specification of a TOS and specification of its
moral duties (if any).[12] I should add that there's no entailment in this

---

[12]That is, specification of its physical and mental properties, including its *teloi*.

sense between a nonteleological description of such a system and its teleological specification. But, *pace* Hume's pervasive skepticism concerning nonlogical necessary connections, this counts for naught against the claim that it's metaphysically necessary that a physical system in a given environment (and perhaps with a given history or causal ancestry) is teleologically ordered in a certain way, or the claim that a system so ordered is, by metaphysical necessity, bound by certain obligations.

We have, moreover, the ability to recognize such necessary connections.[13] It should be sufficient proof of this that we can, simply by examining the physical features and behaviors of oak trees in their environment, discern that oak trees are TOSs with certain natural ends, and that we can, by discovering the natural ends of sensitive beings, discern certain moral truths about how they may and may not be treated, other things being equal. There is a necessary connection—one we easily recognize—between the nature of a small human child and the prima facie duty not to kill it, a connection mediated by the understanding that in killing it we foreclose in the most fundamental and comprehensive sort of way on the realization of that child's natural *teloi*.

Some of the necessary connections between natures and duties aren't so transparent. Indeed, sometimes, it seems, we have a duty to do *better* than what's natural for us; sometimes and in some ways it's clear that our natures are morally *defective*: we fall short—even far short—of the moral ideal. How can a naturalist account for this important, even pervasive, feature of the moral life?

SQUARING MORAL INTUITIONS WITH HUMAN TELEOLOGY

Perhaps the most unsettling difficulty NMR faces comes from the significant disparities between certain enduring and apparently entrenched aspects of human nature and strong intuitions that the ends

---

[13]I claimed earlier that truths like * are conceptual truths. They concern the necessary connection between ends and obligations. Are they, then, conceptually necessary (and hence a priori), or is the necessity metaphysical (and so not knowable a priori)? This is a case, I believe, where conceptual understanding keeps pace with metaphysical necessity. Here metaphysical necessity doesn't rule out knowability a priori.

associated with those aspects ought not be pursued or satisfied. For example, human societies at all times and in all regions display a distinct proclivity for violence, especially toward neighboring societies with whom there may be some competition for resources (or simply because the neighbors are weaker and so easy targets). This sort of aggressiveness seems deeply embedded in the collective human psyche; that would at least suggest that warfare is a natural end toward which that psyche is directed. Indeed, some moralists are quite content to argue that war is, under certain conditions, morally acceptable or even obligatory. They often display an unsurprising but lamentable proclivity for exonerating their own society's participation in warfare and condemning that of their enemies. But for those who are unapologetic bleeding-heart liberals, or even (with respect to this example) pacifists, these arguments ring hollow. We feel the tug of a higher, more rigorous, calling, a calling that is, for many, epitomized by the Sermon on the Mount. How on earth are we to justify moral precepts that require standards that not only move far beyond usual human behavior but often seem positively at odds with our very natures?

Now the theist has an easy explanation for these facts. When God made us, he made us good. In Adam and Eve, in their original condition, nature and the ideals that a good God intended for humanity coincided; the lacuna we now find between them is explained by the Fall. Human will, even though it was created good, had freedom to choose and, somehow suffering temptation, chose disobedience. The consequence was a kind of moral corruption that left in us a knowledge of the good, but an incapacity by our own efforts to meet its standards. How are naturalists to account for this feature of human moral experience?

The first point is a negative one. When making the case for the historical role of religion—especially Judaism and Christianity—in teaching humanity a higher moral awareness, apologists typically cite the Sermon on the Mount and often claim the (alleged) superiority of the laws of Moses to those of contemporary ancient Near Eastern societies. But when apologists—sometimes the same ones[14]—turn their atten-

---

[14]William Lane Craig is a prominent example. See, e.g., Craig, "Is the Islamic Conception of God Morally Inadequate?" *Reasonable Faith*, www.reasonablefaith.org/is-the-islamic

tion to the problem of evil—in particular, to providing an apologetic for some of the horrific actions and commands attributed to God in the Bible—their moral sensibilities assume a decidedly different cast. Some, indeed, seem quite prepared to defend even such things as rape, genocide and the like, so long as they appear to conform to the divine will.[15] A related point is this: for all the talk of the saving grace of the cross, it should come as a surprise to discover the often sordid and massive ways in which the actual behavior of Christians and their denominations throughout the "Christian era" have departed from the stringent dictates of the Sermon, and indeed how voluminous has been the apologetic literature that seeks to soften or set aside those dictates.

I mention these facts not to bludgeon Christians with them but to point out that they themselves must face the difficulties I am now posing for ethical naturalists, especially with respect to the tenor of conscience and behavior of *saved* Christians. Surely, these facts call into question both the efficacy of Christian salvation and the theoretical commitment of Christians historically to the moral principles articulated in the Sermon on the Mount. If it is true that God holds us to a higher standard than our fallen nature can manage, but through his mercy offers a salvation that overcomes that nature, then we should not expect such meager results. Christians may have an explanation, of sorts, for our divided nature—but little evidence to show in favor of their remedy.

But to return to the challenge to naturalists. A first observation concerns the relationship between culture and biology, on the one hand, and of both culture and biology to human nature on the other. Conceding the enormous complexity of the connections between human biology, human nature and culture, there is one overarching feature of our moral situation that cannot be overemphasized. Biological evolution is

---

-conception-of-god-morally-inadequate, versus Craig, "Slaughter of the Canaanites," *Reasonable Faith*, www.reasonablefaith.org/slaughter-of-the-canaanites.

[15]For a rather chilling example of this side of Christian apologetics, see, e.g., some of the essays in Stanley N. Gundry, ed., *Show Them No Mercy: 4 Views on God and Canaanite Genocide* (Grand Rapids: Zondervan, 2003).

a slow process during which psychological adaptations—the development of instinct, affect, social behaviors and intelligence—for millennia more or less kept pace, we may assume, with physical adaptations to environmental challenges. Culture also evolves, and doubtless something akin to natural selection also operates to drive cultural change. But the intelligence and intense sociality conferred on us by our biological history have produced a capacity and a set of incentives for cultural change that have far outpaced in rapidity the ability of our biology to keep up.

To dramatically oversimplify and put the point as bluntly as possible: for some millions of years hominids survived basically by engaging in a hunter-gatherer economy while living in small kin-related bands. Then, some fifty thousand years ago, there began a cultural explosion in which technical innovation, symbolic expression and the size of social units began to grow at exponentially increasing rates. It's not too much to suggest that, so far as our genetic makeup and the social instincts it controls go, we are basically hunter-gatherers who find ourselves born into social unit orders of magnitude larger and more complex than our biological adaptations are designed to handle. With those complexities come new moral questions and new situations in which old moral principles need to applied.

We have this advantage: we are intelligent, more-or-less rational beings. Thus we can reflect upon our moral commitments. We can see, for example, how a certain consistency demands that we universalize or expand the scope of moral commitments that may earlier have embraced a much narrower slice of fellow humanity, and entertain ways of effecting the requisite changes in our behaviors and institutions. This is certainly part of our natural endowment, but so too are atavistic instincts that make putting new insights into practice so dauntingly difficult. In that way, our biology has generated a kind of "conflicted" nature within us.

The point about nature and culture highlights another complexity confronting ethical reflection. How malleable is human nature? How is the distinction between the effects of nature and those of nurture to be drawn, and what role should facts about the effects of nurture—of culture, in particular—play in moral judgment? I've already noted that there is a place in ethics for conventions. Here, however, I'm not concerned about conventions per se, but ways in which culture can affect "who we are"—what our aspirations are, our range of emotional reactions to circumstances and the like.

In my view, it's still our fundamental nature that calls the shots, in the sense of limiting the range of cultural arrangements that can produce human flourishing. Plato already had this insight: the ideal society is one in which the right ordering of the state is coordinate with the right ordering of the soul, and the right ordering of both is a function of natural and universal human ends. Plato proposes an especially simple and elegant schema in which the structure of a tripartite soul is mapped directly onto the tripartite structure of the ideal state. We may doubt Plato's anthropology: here's a paradigm arena for empirical information (whether from common experience and folk psychology or from the social sciences) in the service of moral understanding.

Institutional arrangements fall on a spectrum between those that promote human flourishing and those whose viability clashes strongly with the constraints of human nature. Here are two examples. First, Larry Arnhart has argued that the natural bonds between parents and their children are too strong to permit communal child rearing with no special role for biological parents in the disciplining and nurturing of their offspring.[16] Arnhart cites the failure of Israeli kibbutzim, where this social experiment was tried, as evidence. He may be right: however ideal such an arrangement might seem from a certain ideological perspective, it may be an idea over which Mother Nature has exercised a veto.

Second, polygamy, reviled in most industrial societies, is clearly a viable social institution, one with a long and stable history in many societies. It almost always takes the form of polygyny rather than polyandry. It does not follow, of course, that (other things being equal) it is the, or an, optimal marriage institution. Indeed because, in the usual case of polygyny, it lends itself so easily to exploitation of women, one

---

[16]Larry Arnhart, *Darwinian Natural Right: The Biological Ethics of Human Nature* (Albany, N.Y.: State University of New York Press, 1998).

may argue that a society that institutionalizes it falls on that score short of the human ideal.

Granting that evolution has shaped who we are, I want to press a second point. We should not be too mesmerized by questions about how we came to be what we are when we think about the proper relationship between our natures, our ends and goods, and the ethically obligatory.[17] Rather, we should focus upon *eudaimonia:* what true felicity consists in, for the (generic) individual human being and for human society, and ask what moral prescriptions best reflect those ends and the sorts of means we have for achieving them.

Take pacifism. The pacifist can point out, without fear of being contradicted, that peace is a better condition to be in than a state of war. Thus we ought to pursue the former. The debate is over means. The belligerent will insist that defense of self, kith and kin, by violent means if necessary, is always a right and sometimes the only, or best, way to achieve a just peace. Perhaps that's true, though experience suggests that violence begets violence. The pacifist claims that the cycle can be broken by repaying evil with good, relying on the deeply entrenched human instinct of reciprocity. Who is correct in this debate is, clearly, a matter only to be decided by experience—but the pacifist means have seldom been tried.

Let me reflect on one final case, in which our biological natures seem to oppose a strong (for many) ethical intuition: that we should

---

[17]There's been a good deal of obsession of late with the lessons evolution can supposedly teach us about the proper ends of human nature and their moral relevance (see n. 12 for a discussion of FitzPatrick's view of the matter; also, e.g., Edward O. Wilson and Michael Ruse, "Moral Philosophy as Applied Science," *Philosophy* 61 [1986]: 173-92, and, for counterviews, Christine M. Korsgaard, "Morality and the Distinctiveness of Human Action," in *Primates and Philosophers*, ed. Frans B. M. Waal et al. [Princeton, N.J.: Princeton University Press, 2009], pp. 98-119, and Philip Kitcher's attacks on sociobiology, as in his *Vaulting Ambition* [Cambridge, Mass.: MIT Press, 1985] and "Four Ways of 'Biologicizing' Ethics," in *Conceptual Issues in Evolutionary Biology*, ed. Elliott Sober, 3rd ed. [Cambridge, Mass.: MIT Press, 2006], pp. 575-86). In my own view, recognition of the proto-moral affect and cognitive abilities in primates, especially the great apes and Capuchin monkeys, is of great interest and importance in understanding the moral capacities and limitations of *Homo sapiens*. Still, although it is true that some *teloi* toward which organisms are organized will not be discoverable in the absence of some knowledge of their evolutionary history, it is plainly false that teleological organization is blankly opaque to anyone who lacks such knowledge, or that the *morally relevant teloi* of human beings are in general invisible to those who are ignorant of our evolutionary history.

not willingly cause animal suffering. This intuition runs up hard against the fact that we are by nature omnivores. Killing and the eating of meat are part of our biological heritage. How can an ethical naturalist who shares the intuition that killing innocent creatures is wrong defend vegetarianism?

At the heart of a moral defense of vegetarianism is a key feature of moral thought: universalizability. We recognize that animals have interests, that they can be harmed. Among other things, they can suffer. Moreover, they are innocents: harming them cannot be a matter of exacting retributive justice. Thus, our reasons for harming them can, at best, be purely ones of self-interest. The question then is whether that sort of self-interest can override the infliction of grievous harm on an innocent creature. One indication that we are not convinced that it can is our attitude toward pets. It cannot be merely in virtue of the special relationships we enjoy with our own pet animals that we abhor the notion of killing them for food, for we feel the same way about others' pets and strays that have no such relationship to human beings. It is not my intention to settle this matter here, but only to point out that it pits a practical interest that we have in high-quality protein and gustatory pleasure against a principle of justice demanded by intellectual consistency. As we are at heart and at our best rational creatures, we cannot lightly regard such intellectual demands; a commitment to them lies at the heart of proper fulfillment of our own ends.

THEISTIC VERSUS NATURALISTIC NATURAL LAW THEORIES

The sort of naturalistic moral theory I've presented has, broadly speaking, strong affinities with the natural law tradition, a tradition with roots in Plato and Aristotle, and subsequently developed in a theistic vein by Aquinas, Samuel Clarke, Ralph Cudworth and others. Let's take note of where theistic and naturalistic theories of this kind diverge, as well as what they share.[18]

---

[18]To the extent that a theistic natural law theory provides a role for divine legislation as a component in its account of the binding force of the moral law, it might be regarded a mongrel theory with some divine command theory blood in its veins (as, e.g., Duns Scotus, Suarez, and

Both NMR and theistic natural-law theories (TNLs) take the fundamental moral facts to concern goods and evils. TNLs also usually see these as always goods or evils *for* beings of a given kind. Both view rights and wrongs as determined by goods and evils, though not in narrowly consequentialist ways. Both deny the spirit of Hume's is-ought distinction, because they see teleology built into the very natures of living things, and understand good and evil for creatures to be determined by those creatures' natural ends. What they primarily disagree about is how creatures came by the teleological organization in virtue of which the goods-evils, and rights-wrongs, follow. Secondarily, they may disagree over the means by which it's possible to come to know the moral law and, cosmically speaking, over whether the universe as a whole might have some *telos*. TNL theorists typically hold that we recognized the moral law not only via reason and natural inclination, but also via revelation. It's unclear, however, that the latter offers much epistemic advantage, for two reasons. First, the greatest moral difficulties we face usually involve moral dilemmas, and no set of published rules, however elaborate, can hope to cover even an appreciable portion of cases; God would have to maintain a twenty-four-hour advice service (and few of us are prepared to trust those who think he does). Second, such moral lessons as the Bible does teach hardly inspire confidence: they're a mixed bag, and selective culling would have to appeal to an independent standard.[19] Theists likely will also disagree with naturalists over specific moral norms, because they'll disagree over what's true of, or most essential to, human nature and human flourishing. Characteristically, theists hold that the highest and most comprehensive human end is the love of God; naturalists will, naturally, demur.[20] But there remains a broad arena of agreement,

---

Locke—see Mark Murphy, "The Natural Law Tradition in Ethics," *Stanford Encyclopedia of Philosophy*, http://plato.stanford.edu/entries/natural-law-ethics.

[19]The issue has come in for considerable recent discussion. See, e.g., Gundry, *Show Them No Mercy*; Michael Bergmann, Michael J. Murray and Michael C. Rea, *Divine Evil? The Moral Character of the God of Abraham* (Oxford: Oxford University Press, 2010); and Evan Fales, "Despair, Optimism, and Rebellion," *SecularWeb*, 2007, www.infidels.org/library/modern/evan_fales/despair.html.

[20]There will also likely be disagreement over rather specific moral prohibitions (e.g., sex before marriage, homosexual sex and abortion). Here Christian theists are moved by what they

nevertheless, over what the ends and consequent norms are.

But how much do these differences matter for the ontology—the truth makers—of ethical claims? What do they distinctively imply about ethical facts? In a nutshell: not much. It would commit a genetic fallacy, of sorts, to suppose that what's right and wrong depends, other than causally, on the source of our nature. Having that nature, the ethical facts follow. Insofar then as naturalist and theist can agree over what human nature is—which is itself a matter for empirical investigation—they have a basis for agreement over normative ethics.[21] Thus, were I to become convinced that the theist's God exists, it would not require much of a conceptual overthrow to adopt a TNL theory of ethics; conversely, a theist who begins with a TNL theory and deconverts can quite happily accept NMR.

The upshot is that we may discern certain dialectical symmetries. NMR and TNL theories agree that what matters, for the grounding of moral facts, is that we (and any other rational agents that may exist in the universe) are ITOSs, however such systems may have arisen. As to which of the two alternative etiological hypotheses is true, I put my money on neo-Darwinian evolution for, even though we don't yet understand how original intentionality and purpose arose, we can at least say that (1) there is abundant evidence that favors evolution as a general etiological account of the biological facts, (2) divine creation enjoys no *conceptual* advantage as an explanation of this and (3) neo-Darwinism offers us a genuine explanatory project vis-á-vis the genesis of consciousness and original intentionality, whereas theism has

---

see (rightly or wrongly) as the authority of the Bible and, at least in the latter two cases, in lessons they think (again, rightly or wrongly) can be learned from a direct examination of human nature.

[21] I concede in principle that to the extent that teleology depends on causal history, that sort of disagreement between theists and naturalists could arise. But in practice, I'm not sure this amounts to much. Many theists are prepared to admit that God has "worked" (somehow) through (Darwinian) evolutionary processes to produce human nature. Those who are not may well disagree concerning certain specific issues (e.g., about whether we have been endowed by God with natures that are properly respected only by heterosexual marriage and only by sexual union between married couples, and about whether other arrangements are "disordered"). But they appear mostly to be ignorant of current biology, to say nothing of not having thought through carefully the larger ways in which moral judgments must be sensitive to facts about human sociality—as well as being saddled with a decidedly unsophisticated appreciation of their own canonical traditions of revelation.

little to offer beyond mere assertion that God (somehow) creates beings "in his image."

On the other hand, divine command theories (DCTs) share an assumption with naturalistic error theories (which deny the existence of objective moral truths), for an error theory might agree, in contrast to NMR and TNL theories, that the existence of such truths depends on the existence of a divine being. The error theory disagrees with DCTs over whether such a being exists; a fortiori, it disagrees over the existence of moral truths.

Both DCTs and error theories have a certain intellectual appeal—an appeal that may, however, derive in part from a certain intellectual intuition run amuck. The intuition is that moral norms are universal. It is perhaps not so unnatural to think that they must therefore be written into the very structure of the universe, if they have the kind of status and authority required of morality. But how could they have that kind of authority and universality? Only if God, the Creator and Ruler of the universe, pronounces them as universal law. Since nothing less will do, there aren't "really" any moral laws, absent God. NMR and TLN theories, on the other hand, plump for a more plausible conception of universality, and, for an atheist such as I am, that leaves NMR as the correct view of the matter.

A Naturalist Moral Nonrealism Response

Michael Ruse

AT ONE LEVEL, EVAN FALES AND I are very much on the same side. At another level, I am not sure we could be further apart. Obviously we are very much on the same side inasmuch as we both want to promote a nontheistic, naturalistic view of morality. At the level of descriptive ethics, I don't suppose that there is much that divides us. At the level of metaethics, neither of us wants to go beyond the world and science and so forth in our quest for understanding. And I suspect we also share the conviction that we have succeeded in doing what we set out to do.

How then are we so very far apart? I would say that one of us has crossed the Hume-Kantian divide (me) and the other has not (Fales). I don't mean that in a nasty sense, I really don't. But I think there is a real difference here. I would say, by his own admission—and I don't mean that this slipped out inadvertently, but that Fales proclaims this proudly—Fales is an Aristotelian or at least very much in that tradition. By my own admission—and again I proclaim this proudly—I am a Humean, and I am happy to use Kant to mop up a lot of the problems that Hume left behind.

It comes out most clearly on the matter of the is-ought distinction. Fales denies flatly and absolutely its importance and validity. For me, it is the starting point of my assault on the problems of morality. As I read him, Fales sees ends and subsequent values actually residing, existing independently, out there in the world. To coin a phrase, even if there were no one around in the wood, the acorn would still in some way have the end of making an oak tree, and things like water and sunshine and rabbit droppings would be considered good things in helping to make that end come about. It is part of the acorn's nature to turn into the oak, that is, a value phenomenon, and it is as real as the acorn's oval shape and brown skin and tastiness to pigs. Turning to humans, I take it that Fales wants to say that being moral is just as natural, just as much a matter of ends, for social beings as is the becoming of an oak for the acorn. This isn't ethereal. This is just part of nature. And of course, in both cases, Darwinian evolutionary biology—I don't want to get into an argument about whether Darwinism is the right evolutionary theory, and will assume that we are in harmony on this—is the guide and the means of understanding. Why does the acorn have these features? Because it increases its chances of thriving and reproducing. I am not much up on pig digestion, but perhaps like birds every now and then—having been eaten thanks to its expected tastiness—a particularly tough-skinned acorn goes right through and is deposited in its own little bed of fertilizer. Why are we moral? Because humans who are moral tend to do better than those who are not and are thus more likely to leave offspring.

For me, I am a Cartesian. I think the world is *res extensa*. It is just matter in motion. It has no meaning. It has no values. To quote Richard Dawkins yet again: "In a universe of blind physical forces and genetic replication, some people are going to get hurt, other people are going to get lucky, and you won't find any rhyme or reason in it, nor any justice."[1] Continuing: "As that unhappy poet A. E. Houseman put it: 'For Nature, heartless, witless Nature / Will neither know nor care.' DNA neither knows nor cares. DNA just is. And we dance to its music."[2] I take the distinction between "is" statements and "ought" statements to be one of the fundamental discoveries and premises of philosophical thinking. It is for this reason that although I think evolution can explain why we are moral, it cannot justify it. Whereas I assume that for Fales the justification simply comes as part of the package of his form of Aristotelian naturalism. Once you see that this is the proper way for things to behave, justification is given and more justification is simply not needed.

Or is it? What does it mean to be an Aristotelian in this day and age? Without being too anachronistic, I see two possible answers here. One might go for some kind of full-blooded life force—a real entity that is not necessarily conscious but very truly end directed. This was the option

---

[1]Richard Dawkins, *River Out of Eden: A Darwinian View of Life* (New York: Basic Books, 1995), p. 133.
[2]Ibid.

chosen by the so-called vitalists at the turn of the nineteenth and twentieth centuries. In Germany, there was Hans Driesch with his "entelechies," and in France Henri Bergson with "élans vitaux." A more recent biologist attracted that way was Julian Huxley, the grandson of Charles Darwin's "bulldog," Thomas Henry Huxley. Of course the problem with vitalism is that it is hard to see how a notion like a vital force can be captured—that is, quantified and measured and so forth. What work is it doing and how beyond the motions of molecules? The alternative is to opt for some kind of "organicism," often known as "holism" or (sometimes) as "emergentism." One argues that nature itself is more harmonious than one might think and that (although not designed) it just has a natural tendency to work for the good of organisms. Recently a related version of this kind of thinking has been known as "complexity" theory, and its supporters, like the theoretical biologist Stuart Kauffman (1995), talk in terms of "order for free." The trouble with this kind of thinking is that so very often order is not free. Murphy's Law holds throughout—things go wrong, things mess up and rot or rust, and sophisticated complexity is just not the normal way of the world. Aristotelianism in its day was a noble tradition, but like Christianity (to which Aristotelianism gave so much) it is an exhausted paradigm.

So how then do I explain the teleology, the ends, that as a Darwinian I see in nature, because I certainly think that the tough skin of the acorn serves the ends of the reproduction of individual members of oak species, just as being nice to babies serves the ends of our reproduction? As I said, I turn to Kant here, especially to the Kant of the third *Critique*. I think that we see the world "as if" designed and go from there. It is not designed—at least it is not designed as far as science is concerned—but we treat it as if it were. As it happens, Kant didn't think we could go any further. "We can boldly say that it would be absurd for humans even to make such an attempt or to hope that there may yet arise a Newton who could make comprehensible even the generation of a blade of grass according to natural laws that no intention has ordered; rather, we must absolutely deny this insight to human beings."[3] It was

---

[3]Immanuel Kant, *Critique of the Power of Judgment*, trans. Paul Guyer and Eric Matthews (Cambridge: Cambridge University Press, 2001), p. 271.

Darwin's genius to come up with natural selection and show how de-sign-like effects could be explained naturally. But for Kant and Dar-win, the design—the ends—is not to be found in the world but imputed to it. (Both Kant and Darwin—at least at the time of writing the *Ori-gin*—thought there was a Designer, but it could not be part of science.)

Of course ultimately I don't think there are any ends. You can have ends for individual organisms, but I don't think overall that organisms have any purpose. They just are, like everything else. I am a mechanist. The world is like a machine, and even though the earlier thinkers thought God was involved in his creation, in the words of one of the greatest historians of the scientific revolution, God now is "a retired engineer."[4] At the risk of being a bore, I say again, "The universe we observe has precisely the properties we should expect if there is, at bot-tom, no design, no purpose, no evil and no good, nothing but blind, pitiless indifference."[5] You either get ethics out of or despite this, as I think you can, or you don't get ethics at all.

So who is right, Ruse or Fales? I suspect that there is ultimately no definitive answer on this one. It is all a bit like sexual orientation. No amount of good advice is going to make anyone change. What I would say however is that our debate is really not something that should be done in isolation. I am part of a philosophical tradition. He is part of a philosophical tradition. For better or for worse—I would say very much for better—my tradition is the one that has ruled in science for the past almost five hundred years and has been incredibly successful. His has not. I don't think we philosophers have to be led by the nose by the scientists, but we should take note. I'll leave it at that.

---

[4]E. J. Dijksterhuis, *The Mechanization of the World Picture* (Oxford: Oxford University Press, 1961), p. 40.
[5]Dawkins, *River Out of Eden*, p. 133.

A Moral Essentialism Response

Keith E. Yandell

> What is right and good is so always *for* beings of a certain kind. . . .
>   Might there not be intrinsic goods and evils that are not good or
> bad *for* any being as such, but simply good or bad *simpliciter*—things
> or states of affairs that are such that, as it were, it is simply a good or
> bad thing absolutely that the universe contain them? Perhaps it's
> good that the universe contain beings of a certain sort—intelligent
> beings, for example, or social beings. But I'll not pursue this matter
> here.—Evan Fales (pp. 13, 17/n4)

NATURALISM

Naturalism has two relevant senses. One concerns metaphysics. Professor Fales expresses his metaphysical naturalism in this succinct manner: there are no disembodied persons. Thus there is no God, no soul that can outlast the body, and no mind of any other sort that is distinct from any and all bodies. The price for this metaphysical naturalism is steep. This rules out even saying there are immaterial things—souls that are embodied in and distinct from human bodies—that do not outlast the life of those bodies. Theism is rejected, as is the idealism of Bishop Berkeley, for which sensory experience, which we take to be of bodies extended in space, is really conscious experience that has color, shape, tactility and so forth—content that is private to the nonphysical mind that has it. Rejected also is the dualism of Descartes, for which human beings are embodied immaterial minds capable of surviving the demise of their bodies.

The other sense of *naturalism* concerns ethics. There are descriptive properties such as *being round, weighing thirty pounds, being six feet tall.* There are normative properties such as *being good, being bad, being obligatory, being right, being wrong.* Metaphysical naturalism entails this constraint concerning human beings: (N) *There is no human being and no human property whose existence lacks a neo-Darwinian explanation.* In

Falesean terms, any property (or thing) explicable in neo-Darwinian terms is a natural property. For Fales both descriptive and normative properties are natural properties. So it is not required that one must reduce to the other. Fales is an ethical naturalist whose position is constrained by neo-Darwinian metaphysics. (N), of course, is a metaphysical, not a biological, claim.

NATURALISTIC ETHICS

Remembering that Fales sets aside the question of whether there is anything that has intrinsic worth, his naturalistic ethic entails that a thing's flourishing is good for that thing, and every good is good *for* something. The former claim is offered in the context of things that have natures and it being at least possible that there are paradigm cases of a kind of thing—an instance in which the potential unique to being of its kind is realized. Doctors, veterinarians, gardeners and farmers are able to identify prime specimens of various species, and people without special expertise can identify flourishing items with less accuracy. Some such things are as observable as the white of an egg or the light of a star. For any item that is a member of a kind, its good is to flourish as that *sort* of thing. Thus the criterion for goodness, if not the meaning of *good*, varies from kind to kind. More precisely, *good* has a general sense, where "*x* is good" means "*x* is flourishing in its kind," and "*x*'s flourishing in its kind" is analyzable without remainder into *x*'s having the right natural properties.

Fales holds that goodness is objective. What is good is not a function of what we think is good, and it does not change as our opinions change. What is good for something, Fales explains, is a function of the nature of that thing, which is not up to us. The things in question are what Fales calls "teleologically ordered systems" (TOS): systems that naturally (because of their nature or essence) so operate as to realize one or more ends. A clock is a TOS, but its status as such is contributed by a clockmaker; its teleological status is extrinsic. An oak is a TOS, and its teleological status is intrinsic. There is something toward which it tends such that if it reaches that end, it flourishes as what it is. The range of things to which "good for" can properly apply is the set of teleologically ordered systems whose teleological ordering is intrinsic and natural—artifacts are not in that range.

It seems to me, though, that Fales's naturalist moral realism is not (yet) an ethic. It needs two additions, which can be presented in two steps.

Step one. A world containing nothing higher than plant life could have a massive number of species, each of which flourishes despite nary a thing being intrinsically good. Such a world could be chock full of "good for" without a single thing being good, *simpliciter*. A variety of entities can qualify as being good without any of them being morally good. "For goodness" is neither identical to nor guarantees intrinsic goodness or moral goodness.

We can explain the force of this in these terms. At least as used here, *presupposes* has this sense: proposition Q presupposes proposition P if and only if, should P be false, then so is Q. Fales's view, to be an ethic, requires some such addition as this: for all (or at least some) x, *that x flourish is good. Good* here is not "good for something else"; it means "good for its own sake." Something must have intrinsic goodness.

Suppose there are three things, x, y and z, each of which is "good for"—x for x^*, y for y^*, and z for z^*. What about x^*, y^* and z^*? Are they good? If so, for Falesean "ethics," each is good for something else. In principle, this can lead to a series in which nothing has value for its own sake. Even if x^* is good for y^*, y^* for z^* and z^* for x^*, in a circle of extrinsic worth, still nothing has intrinsic value. Appeal to the point that for Fales *being good for* is objective will not help. Something can have objective worth that has only extrinsic value in virtue of being contributory to the flourishing of something else. "Being good for x," even if x is a TOS, need not matter much. X isn't much of a good if x does not matter much. So far, there need be nothing morally good at all. Fales of course is aware of this issue and does not pursue it.

The reason for this assumption concerning intrinsic goodness is to answer this question: Why should the fact that something is good for x be of value significance if x itself has no worth? The net effect, if this is right, is that the matter into which Fales does not inquire is crucial for his position—it is crucial for naturalist moral realism that (at least) some things have intrinsic worth.

The traditional context in which teleological value theory has been developed has contained the claim that *being* and *goodness* are (among other things) so related that insofar as an item has the former, it also has the latter. This entails that every existent has some intrinsic worth. Falesean ethics requires, I suggest, that any intrinsically teleological system contains things of such worth. A world in which lots of things that possess no intrinsic worth flourish arguably is a world on which ethics has no purchase.

It is worth pointing out that there is another matter that points toward a presupposition of the intrinsic worth of at least some TOS. Fales holds that a TOS has built into it that it undergoes certain processes and we can observe that it has this feature. In some such cases we also see that its being so ordered binds us to certain obligations. He refers in this context to nonlogically necessary connections between ends and obligations. For example, we can know in general what a child's flourishing requires, and that maiming or murdering the child will prevent that from occurring. Fales then claims that there is a nonlogically necessary connection between the child having a *telos* (end) and our having an obligation not to thwart that end. He adds that we can see that this is true. *Pace* Fales, however, if neither the child itself nor anything of which the child is a part has intrinsic worth, why should there be any obligation to be recognized? In contrast to Ruse, Fales does not want merely to talk about the phenomenology of obligation—just to say that we, uniquely among creatures, have a special feeling that we should do or refrain from doing something. For Ruse, this feeling is deceptive though important since the illusion that there are obligations is socially so useful. For Fales, we actually have these obligations and do not just feel that we have them. There are necessary connections between our encountering many a TOS in daily life and our being obligated not to bring it about that a TOS cannot flourish. I suggest that an ethic restricted to "goodness for," such as naturalist moral realism, cannot bear the weight of this commitment. Obligations require more than extrinsic value in that to which we have them.

Step two. Talk of obligations has already brought in the second addition that Fales needs. Obligations do not exist without there being moral agents to have them. It is very widely recognized that persons have obligations to one another (however much one believes that our obligations do not stop with persons). Moral agents are conscious and self-aware beings who can act for ends (reasons). They not only qualify for membership in the TOS society but *intentionally* act so as to bring about their own flourishing. They seek ends other than their own flourishing. They are obligated to do this. On a Falesean account we can see nonlogically necessary connections between (for example) persons flourishing and an obligation at least not to destroy or maim people so as to prevent their flourishing. However, if persons have no intrinsic worth, why think we have obligations to them? (A possible answer is that humans are parts of something "bigger" that has intrinsic worth though individual humans lack it. The tactic of ascribing inherent worth only to artificial or natural collectives has not distinguished itself, morally speaking.) The presence of moral agents in a world introduces moral worth into that world. It also requires intrinsic goodness. Falesean naturalist moral realism lacks these additions and so does not add up to an ethic.

ORIGIN AND WORTH

Another strand of Falesean thought is relevant. An important part of naturalist moral realism is that the properties something has determines its worth, quite independent of how it came to have them. The value of being a human person is the same whether human persons came to be only from neo-Darwinian causes or whether God creates them (even if God uses some neo-Darwinian causes in the process). The claim is that it matters not how we got here—our worth is a function of what features we have, independent of how we got them. Is this to be true only of what we are *good for?* Aristotelian, Christian and Kantian ethics all hold that persons are of intrinsic worth. Theism will ascribe properties to persons that Fales does not: being created by God, being capable of worshiping an actual God, being made in God's image and the like. But there is a wide range of properties that Fales and theists will ascribe to persons: for example, those necessary for doing science and philosophy, for having obligations, for acting from motives and the like. There seems to me no Falesean ground for ascribing intrinsic worth to persons, as do those who agree with him on at least a significant subset of the properties that Fales ascribes to them. As he claims, though, Fales shares considerable common ground with theists as to the worth of human persons independent of disagreement as to their source. A theist can grant that, had human persons come to exist without God's actions, they still would have intrinsic worth, even the worth that the theist ascribes to them, while denying that this did, or even could, happen. This too supports the idea that Falesean "ethics" is at least friendly to the idea of persons having intrinsic worth.

HISTORICAL ADDENDUM

Both Professors Ruse and Fales refer to Hume and not being able to infer from a descriptive proposition to a normative proposition. Put formally, the idea is this: for any descriptive proposition D and any normative proposition N, D does not entail N. Hume, however, says a claim of the form "It is good that A be done" means, or is reducible to, "When taking a disinterested point of view, we approve of A being done." Since the latter is also descriptive, claims about what is good or bad turn out to be (identical or reducible to) claims about psychological states had by people who make disinterested (unbiased) judgments. You can deduce an "ought" from an "is" provided you recognize that an "ought" statement really is a particular kind of "is" statement—not a claim about the external world but a claim about attitudes felt by unbiased persons (see Hume's *A Treatise Concerning Human Nature* 3.1.1).

I close with a brief comparison between Hume's views and those of Ruse and Fales. Hume's position relates to Ruse's as follows: (1) neither believes in nonnatural (nonempirical) moral properties or facts; (2) both ascribe to us a certain feeling that motivates right action, though for Hume it is approval and for Ruse it is a sense of obligation; (3) for Hume, the feeling of approval (an "impression of reflection") *constitutes* the rightness of the action approved, whereas for Ruse the feeling of obligation motivates us to act in accord with propensities whose explanation is purely neo-Darwinian, and there is only a feeling of obligation without any actual obligations.

Hume's view compares to Fales in a different manner. In contrast to Hume, Fales believes that (1) there are necessary connections that are not captured by formal logic. He also holds the un-Humean position that (2) we can "see" that we have obligations due to mind-independent features of the world. It is unclear to me how the actual obligations that we have are natural properties—properties that have a neo-Darwinian explanation. It is one thing to endeavor to explain in neo-Darwinian fashion how we come to have certain feelings, though there is also a Kantian and a theistic explanation of our sense of obligations. It is something else to offer a neo-Darwinian explanation about our actually having obligations.

A Moral Particularism Response

Mark D. Linville

PROFESSOR FALES'S CHARACTERISTICALLY LUCID and carefully argued defense of naturalistic moral realism deserves to be ranked among the several seminal defenses of ethical naturalism that have appeared within the past two or three decades. His view enjoys, I think, a great deal of plausibility, and his supporting arguments are compelling. But I am not ultimately convinced, and so will attempt to say why.

The view offered has moral values and obligations ultimately derived from certain objective and observable facts about the nature of humans and other creatures with moral standing. However we got here, whether created from the dust in a day or evolved from the slime over the eons, there is, it seems, such a thing as human nature. Given that nature, there are natural human ends—of varying importance to our well-being—that can be helped or hindered. Generally, it is a good thing to further human ends so as to promote human flourishing, and we are sometimes morally obligated to help. And it is, all else equal, a bad thing to hinder such ends, and we have moral obligations to refrain. This much seems undeniable for anyone but the entrenched moral skeptic like Professor Ruse when in a philosophical mood. However, I am not certain that Fales is entitled to such moral beliefs given the metaphysics of naturalism.

Fales introduces the notion of a "teleologically organized system" (TOS) and explains that this is anything that is organized so as to have one or more ends or purposes. While the general notion includes things like computers, whose ends are imputed, his concern is over those TOSs with intrinsic ends—ITOSs—humans, in particular. Fales excuses himself from the task of offering an analysis of teleological properties in terms of nonteleological ones, but insists that the world is replete with examples of ITOSs. Presumably, anything capable of insisting (or denying) that there are ITOSs *is* one, so there is no argument there. The question is whether a naturalist like Fales can account for this fact. As he anticipates, some will doubt that a successful naturalistic account of such things is possible and will capitalize on the yawning explanatory gap when it comes to original intentionality. The point is not merely that no such account has yet to be offered—though I think none has, and, in fact, such reductionist programs appear to be mired in a slough of despond. Rather, it is the suspicion that the account would require more things in the world than are dreamed of in the naturalist's philosophy. Arguably, the consistent naturalist will be an eliminativist regarding such things as conscious purposes or beliefs. Alex Rosenberg appears to be in the minority among naturalists in his assertion that "the mind is no more a purpose-driven system than anything else in nature," and, again, "the brain no more has original intentionality than anything else does."[1] My own assessment is that Rosenberg's "disenchantment" is the result of taking naturalism seriously. It is common knowledge that naturalists have no place for teleology at the cosmic level. But, arguably, a consistent version of naturalism also implies that my decision to order a cheeseburger is the product of causes that had no prevision of the end they were achieving. If there are ultimately no *teloi* then neither are there ITOSs, nor any footing for Fales's brand of ethics.

In anticipation of this criticism, Fales delivers a kind of *tu quoque*: What has the theist to offer as an alternative explanation? If I say that God confers original intentionality, precisely *how* does he do so? The question has implications similar to a point made by Peter van Inwagen, who, after observing that the physicalist has a hard problem explaining how physical things can think, notes that the problem is no less hard if we posit *non*physical thinking things. Alvin Plantinga has replied by arguing that, on dualism, an immaterial self is simple, not consisting of parts. And thought is an essential, basic and immediate activity of selves in the way that spin and negative charge are basic properties of electrons. Where the naturalist is faced with the daunting challenge of explaining how an assemblage of nonthinking parts can think, Plantinga maintains that on dualism, "There isn't any *how* about it" when it comes to the

---

[1]Alex Rosenberg, "The Disenchanted Naturalist's Guide to Reality," *On the Human*, November 9, 2009, http://onthehuman.org/2009/11/the-disenchanted-naturalists-guide-to-reality.

question of thinkers and their thoughts.[2] The answer to Fales's demand
for a theistic analysis of original intentionality, then, is that if anything
like dualism is true there just *isn't* any analysis. Despite his protest to the
contrary, saying that God "did it" by creating a rational soul is no more
problematic than saying that electrons are endowed with spin and negative charge just by virtue of existing.

Perhaps this will strike some as an instance of special pleading. As
Tom Clark observes in his review of a recent theistic critique of naturalism, this seems all too easy—like pushing the "easy button" featured
in a series of office supply advertisements. But the dualist has an unlikely and unwitting ally in answering Tom Clark: Tom Clark. In the
same review he opens by asserting that whatever explanatory problems
naturalists may face, the dualist is much worse off. Any root "ontological divide" that splits reality into two categorically distinct sorts of
things—souls and bodies, natural and supernatural—poses a barrier to
explaining how such things can interact in any lawlike way. He adds,
"Anti-naturalists, committed to the existence of something *beyond* nature, are perhaps logically barred from showing us clearly how the
world, split in two, works. The very idea of a cogent, transparent *super-
naturalistic* explanation of a phenomenon seems self-contradictory."[3]

Apparently, Clark thinks that he has here offered a significant criticism of any and all such dualisms. But dualists such as Plantinga might
wish to thank Clark for drawing out one of the clear implications of
their view. If anything like dualism is true, then *by definition* there just
isn't any mechanistic explanation of such interaction to be had. Pointing out that the dualist is thus "logically barred" from offering the sort
of explanation that is sought by the naturalist is simply to point out that
dualism is not naturalism, and that is hardly a criticism. If the very
nature of dualism imposes a logical barrier to offering such analyses, it
should not come as a surprise if none is forthcoming. Such "barriers"
occur at any juncture in one's view of things where brute facts or relations or basic properties or actions are posited, which is just here for the

---

[2]Alvin Plantinga and Michael Tooley, *Knowledge of God* (Oxford: Blackwell, 2008), pp. 58-59.
[3]Tom Clark, "No Competition for Naturalism: The Poverty of Supernatural Explanations,"
Naturalism.org, www.naturalism.org/competition.htm.

theist and dualist. The naturalist too must posit such things. Chesterton once said that we cannot explain why pumpkins beget only pumpkins and not, say, giraffes or alligators. We may think this foolish because we have now cracked the pumpkin genome and can offer a careful analysis of pumpkin reproduction. But this is just to kick the pumpkin down the road, so to speak, because at each new level of finer-grained explanation we may ask the same question. The logical terminus is a point at which the answer to the question But why does *this* produce only *that*? is It just does. Indeed, science's Holy Grail is a final explanation where one is "logically barred" from offering more. Like it or not, even—and *especially*—an ideal physics ultimately bows to what, from its own perspective, is a mystery.

Beyond all of this, is a naturalist like Professor Fales entitled to affirm a variety of moral realism? It is hard to see why his overall commitments do not lend themselves more toward the moral skepticism or nihilism of Professor Ruse. There is substantial agreement between the two on a number of salient details. Both, of course, are committed to evolutionary naturalism. Both believe that human morality has taken its present form largely as a result of the actual selection pressures at work on our remote ancestors. Both allow—as Darwin allowed—that human morality might have been significantly different had the circumstances of human evolution been relevantly different. Both would affirm that the range of "acceptable" behavior is restricted by the nature bequeathed us. Ruse suggests that our psychology is just too strong to permit us to forsake morality—at least, not without some protest from conscience. Similarly, Fales believes that "it is our fundamental nature that calls the shots," so that not just any cultural arrangement will be acceptable. Presumably, both would agree with George Santayana's claim that "It is in reference to . . . constitutional interests that things are 'really' good or bad."[4] Santayana was a relativist and an "ethical skeptic,"[5] and Ruse thinks none of this is reason to suppose that ethics

---

[4]George Santayana, *Winds of Doctrine and Platonism and the Spiritual Life* (New York: Harper, 1957), p. 146.

[5]Though he was measuring his view against a Moorean nonnaturalism, which he might have thought the only option for the moral realist.

is anything more than "an illusion fobbed off on us by our genes in order to get us to cooperate."

Why, then, does Fales have a different appraisal? His answer is that whether something is good or bad for creatures of a given nature is a discoverable fact about the natural world. I grant this. But how shall we move from this fact to a robust account of ethics? We have the ability to help or hinder the flourishing of a vast variety of creatures. The mosquito's purposes would be served nicely were Professor Fales to serve up his forearm for a feast. But he tells us that he has lethal intentions when one is prowling nearby. On the other hand, he thinks there is an obvious and necessary connection between the nature of a human child and our duty not to kill it. But insect and infant are equally possessed of *teloi* that are respectively "foreclosed" by insecticide or homicide. Why are there prima facie duties regarding the latter but not the former? Presumably, he would say that the child has moral standing whereas the mosquito does not. But why? The only answer that I can discern is that morality is chiefly about our treatment of our fellow human beings, and this is due to our inherited psychology as social creatures. It is not good for man to be alone. Social relationships lie at the very core of our personhood, and so rank high among our ultimate ends. Because of this, a concern for distributive justice is embedded there, and, we learn, such virtues as justice are their own reward.[6] And because of this, one of our chief aims should be "social flourishing."

Unless there is more to be said, I cannot see how this rises above the observation that as a result of our evolutionary heritage we are wired to

---

[6]Though I think that justice *is* its own reward, I am unhappy with this as an answer to the question of moral motivation. Why should I refrain from raping, pillaging and plundering like a pirate? More to the point, what is it about such acts that *makes* them wrong? The plausible answer is that *people* ought not to be raped, pillaged or plundered. That is, we have *direct duties* to people so that they would be *wronged* by such treatment. "Justice is its own reward," by itself, falls short of this. So does "Rape is not the sort of act that is characteristically committed by a person of excellent character." My concern here is similar to my objection in my main essay to standard accounts of divine command morality. Surely there is more to the wrongness of rape than the observation that it displeases God. In that case the only *direct* duties indicated are to God. The victim figures in as the object of *indirect* duties *regarding* her—a structure of explanation that is shared by explanations of the wrongness of, say, vandalism. For more on this, see Mark D. Linville, "The Moral Argument" in *The Blackwell Companion to Natural Theology*, ed. J. P. Moreland and William Lane Craig (Oxford: Blackwell, 2009).

like people and loathe mosquitoes. But it seems to me that this signals a departure from the realm of objective and discoverable facts. Shall we suppose that the moral property of *having moral standing* is either identical to or supervenes upon the property of *being valued by people*, or the like? One might have thought that the question of moral standing turns upon the possession of certain properties, such as rationality or autonomy or sentience or even the property of being an ITOS. But *being valued* is no more a property of anything than *being Norman's favorite number* is a property of the number 7, alongside *being prime*. This would appear to make the property of moral standing *mind dependent*. And since obligations are directed at things with moral standing, the resulting ethic would appear to be subjective. How is any of this an advance on Ruse? It seems to me that what is needed is a notion of value that is not reducible to *good for*. We ought to value certain things because they are *valuable*.

Convince me that human persons are possessed of dignity in the sense that Kant had in mind and that I believe is implied on Christian theism, and, assuming that I am a person of good will, I will wish to learn what is *good for* them. But then it will be the former sort of value rather than the latter that anchors moral obligation. I fail to find anything like this in Fales's account, and I am afraid that without it there is no way to ground the connection between ends and obligations that Fales thinks he sees. He has asserted the connection. He may reassert it if he wishes. But without a richer moral context, he is in the position of the tourist who asked directions to Millinocket and was told "*You cahn't get theyah from heeah.*"

2

Naturalist Moral Nonrealism

Michael Ruse

I AM A NONBELIEVER. I describe myself as an agnostic or a skeptic, but in truth I am pretty atheistic about the basic claims of Christianity. Many of my good Christian friends think, therefore, that either I have no morality at all or if I do I am being insincere to my more basic beliefs. I find this somewhat surprising and a little discomfiting, because I have never thought of myself as a moral madman. Just like other people, I love my family and my children. I am friendly toward babies and other small animals. I help little old ladies cross the road. When somebody comes around with the collecting box, my hand goes straight into my pocket to find my spare change. What then is my morality really, and how do I justify it?[1] And how does it fit with my program of reconciling science and religion?

PRELIMINARIES

Let me start the discussion with a philosophical distinction and then with a matter of scientific fact. The philosophical distinction I want to

---

[1]I have been arguing this position now for thirty years, although I don't think I have changed essential parts of my case. Earlier expositions include Michael Ruse, *Taking Darwin Seriously: A Naturalistic Approach to Philosophy* (Oxford: Blackwell, 1986); *Evolutionary Naturalism: Selected Essays* (London: Routledge, 1994); and my contributions to Michael Ruse, ed., *Philosophy After Darwin: Classic and Contemporary Readings* (Princeton, N.J.: Princeton University Press, 2009). Expositions of my thinking about the science and religion relationship include Michael Ruse, *Can a Darwinian Be a Christian? The Relationship Between Science and Religion* (Cambridge: Cambridge University Press, 2001); *The Evolution-Creation Struggle* (Cambridge, Mass.: Harvard University Press, 2005); and *Science and Spirituality: Making Room for Faith in the Age of Science* (Cambridge: Cambridge University Press, 2010).

make, one which I think is generally accepted by those engaged in inquiry about morality, is between what is known as "substantive" or "normative" ethics, and "metaethics." By substantive ethics I mean questions about what one should do. Should one help one child over another? Is one obligated to give half of one's income to Oxfam? If war is declared, does one have an obligation to join the armed forces and fight? By metaethics I mean questions about the support or foundations of ethics. Why should I do what I should do? Is it because of the will of God? Is it because of the way the world is made? Is there in fact any support or foundation for morality? I think this is a good division to make, and I shall let it guide the following discussion.

The matter of scientific fact with which I start this discussion is that evolution is true. Organisms, living and dead, including us humans, are the end product of a long, slow, natural process of development from very primitive forms, probably ultimately from inorganic matter. I accept also the central Darwinian mechanism of natural selection to explain evolution, including evolution of human beings. Darwin argued that more organisms are born than can survive and reproduce, and that this leads to a struggle for existence. Combine this with naturally occurring variation, and in each generation you will have a winnowing between the winners (or the fit) and the losers (or the unfit).

It was Darwin's brilliant insight, in his *Origin of Species* (1859), to see that the variations of the winners will, on average, have played an important role in their possessors' success. So not only will there be change, but this will be change of a particular kind. Organic features will be design-like, aimed at helping survival and reproduction. Thus, in the language of biologists, this means, I believe, that the most important and pervasive aspect of the organic world is that it is adapted. The parts of organisms serve the ends of survival and reproduction. In the context of this discussion, therefore, I argue that human features are adaptations—this includes both physical features like hands and eyes and the genitalia, and psychological and mental features like beliefs, emotions and moral sentiments. Like all Darwinians, I recognize that natural selection is not all-powerful. I do not, however, think that this recognition is of great significance at this moment.[2]

Now using the philosophical distinction to structure the discussion, and accepting the fact that I believe the most important thing we can know about human beings is that we are not the creation of a good God on the sixth day but the end product of a long, slow process of natural selection, let us inquire into my thinking about morality. We begin with substantive ethics and then go on to metaethics.

SOCIAL DARWINISM

Now, at once many people will think that they can anticipate both the general outline and the details of my thinking about ethics. After all, at least since the time that Charles Darwin published his *Origin of Species*, there have been enthusiasts for so-called evolutionary ethics. It is today better known as "Social Darwinism," and much has been written on this topic. As it happens, although I do not think that the position I endorse is particularly new, it is certainly not identical with Social Darwinism. Nevertheless, it will be useful to begin detailed discussion with a brief overview of Social Darwinism, because then I can use it as a foil to articulate the philosophical position on morality that I do endorse.[3]

As many scholars have pointed out, although the movement is known as Social Darwinism, in major respects it owes far more to Charles Darwin's fellow English evolutionist Herbert Spencer than to the author of the *Origin*. This at once, it is believed, gives us the clue to the basic substantive ethical claims of the traditional evolutionary ethicists. Spencer, as is well known, was an enthusiast for *laissez-faire* economic policies. He thought that the state should have a minimal role in people's lives, and that natural market forces should prevail.[4] Since Spencer

---

[2]I give the history of Darwin's theory in Michael Ruse, *The Darwinian Revolution: Science Red in Tooth and Claw*, 2nd ed. (Chicago: University of Chicago Press, 1999), and discuss modern thinking about the theory in Michael Ruse, *Darwinism and Its Discontents* (Cambridge: Cambridge University Press, 2006), and *Charles Darwin* (Oxford: Blackwell, 2008). I discuss the human aspects of evolution in much detail in Michael Ruse, *The Philosophy of Human Evolution* (Cambridge: Cambridge University Press, 2011).

[3]For a full account of Social Darwinism and some pertinent extracts, see Ruse, ed., *Philosophy After Darwin*.

[4]Herbert Spencer, *Social Statics; Or the Conditions Essential to Human Happiness Specified and the First of them Developed* (London: J. Chapman, 1851).

undoubtedly endorsed the Darwinian beliefs about the struggle for existence, it is thought that in his system there is therefore a happy parallel between unrestricted competition in the organic world and unrestricted competition in the human, cultural world. Widows and children to the wall, and may big business win!

As it happens, although there is some truth in this general belief, it is only part of Spencer's own thinking, and by no means representative of others who have likewise been labeled Social Darwinians.[5] For a start, Spencer was very selective in his beliefs about competition, both in the organic world and in the social world. He believed that there could be a great deal of cooperation among organisms; likewise, he believed that there could be cooperation among humans. In particular, he was very much opposed to unrestrained competition between nations, believing that this tended to set up trade barriers. He wanted unrestricted free trade and saw strife as antithetical to this end. Furthermore, Spencer and his followers, who included some of the leading American industrialists of the day, including Andrew Carnegie and John D. Rockefeller, tended to stress the success of the winners rather than the inadequacies of the losers.[6] This influenced their social thinking. For instance, Andrew Carnegie is well known for his sponsorship of public libraries. He intended these to be places where the poor-but-gifted child could go and self-educate. Thus the talented would rise to the top. There is little in this vision about competition and loss.

The point I'm trying to make is that even if I were to take Spencer as the touchstone for my thinking about substantive ethics, there is historically no reason why I should automatically accept exclusively the *laissez-faire* view of human culture. This conclusion is confirmed again and again as one spreads one's gaze out and looks at other people, from the time of Darwin on, who have argued for an evolutionary basis to substantive ethical thinking. For instance, Darwin's contemporary and codiscoverer of natural selection, Alfred Russel Wallace, was an ardent

[5]See, for example, Herbert Spencer, *The Data of Ethics* (London: Williams and Norgate, 1879); and R. J. Richards, *Darwin and the Emergence of Evolutionary Theories of Mind and Behavior* (Chicago: University of Chicago Press, 1987).
[6]C. E. Russett, *Darwin in America: The Intellectual Response 1865-1912* (San Francisco: Freeman, 1976).

socialist. In the name of evolution he argued that we should cooperate and that basically the state should run all the major institutions.[7] Then a little later there was the Russian anarchist Prince Peter Kropotkin, who argued that all organisms have a tendency toward mutual aid.[8] On the basis of this, he promoted an anarchistic view of society, where there is basically no government and everything is decided on the individual or the village level.

In the twentieth century we find evolutionary ethicists running the gamut from Julian Huxley, the grandson of Darwin's great supporter Thomas Henry Huxley, who argued for massive state welfare projects,[9] to the Harvard ant specialist and sociobiologist Edward O. Wilson, who argues that humans have grown in symbiotic relationship with nature and that therefore the ultimate biological ethical imperative is to promote biodiversity.[10] He would have us put our energies into saving the Brazilian rainforests.

NATURAL SELECTION AND ALTRUISM

If history is no great guide, what then do I believe, and am I being false to my evolutionary principles in so believing? As I explained right at the beginning, to be honest I don't have anything particularly innovative to say about the nature of substantive ethics, at least based on my own feelings and actions. Along with most people, I think we have special obligations to our family, but please do not conclude that I deny having obligations and duties to friends, workmates and others in our society. In fact, I believe I think along with most people that I have obligations to all human beings, although I would be the first to admit that I infrequently, if ever, live up to what I sometimes proclaim. Like most people I also have fairly strong feelings about specific moral issues, for instance abortion, capital punishment and the rights of women and gays. I recognize, however, that these feelings are somewhat mixed, not in the sense of being wavering but in being deter-

---

[7]Alfred Russel Wallace, *Studies: Scientific and Social* (London: Macmillan, 1900).

[8]Peter Kropotkin, *Mutual Aid: A Factor in Evolution* (Boston: Extending Horizons Books, 1902).

[9]Julian S. Huxley, *Evolutionary Ethics* (Oxford: Oxford University Press, 1943).

[10]Edward O. Wilson, *Biophilia* (Cambridge, Mass.: Harvard University Press, 1984).

mined and informed by what I believe about matters of empirical fact. For instance, I think that gays should have the same rights as everyone else, including the right to get married if they so wish. I recognize that this is not what one might call a pure moral, emotional feeling, but based at least in part on my belief that homosexuals are essentially no different from heterosexuals, that they are not intentionally going with a nonmajority lifestyle, and that as members of society they offer no particular threats.[11]

The next question, then, is whether these beliefs of mine are consistent with my full-blooded commitment to Darwinian evolutionary theory, and whether indeed there is reason to think that they might be products of the Darwinian mechanism of natural selection. In other words, are my substantive moral beliefs adaptations or not? In the *Origin of Species*, Darwin himself recognized that although the struggle for existence can lead to open conflict, it does not necessarily do so. Often one can get more out of life by cooperating rather than by fighting. This is fairly obvious when we think about it. Suppose there is some desirable resource, let us say a freshly killed animal which is a major source of protein. Two rivals might well do much better by deciding to share the booty than fighting over it. There's probably enough for both of them, and by sharing there is no risk of losing a battle and thus incurring physical harm.

In the last half-century we have seen more advances in the field of social behavior than in just about any other area of evolutionary studies. Starting in the 1960s, with the realization that mushy theories about how cooperation or "altruism" will emerge naturally from the evolutionary process are simply false, Darwinian evolutionists have taken seriously the task of explaining such cooperation. Thanks particularly to the work of the English biologists William Hamilton and John Maynard Smith and the American biologists George C. Williams and Robert Trivers, we now have several models explaining animal altruism.[12] Likely the most powerful account is "kin selection," which is

---

[11]Michael Ruse, *Homosexuality: A Philosophical Inquiry* (Oxford: Blackwell, 1988).
[12]William D. Hamilton, "The Genetical Evolution of Social Behaviour," *Journal of Theoretical Biology* 7 (1964): 1-52; John Maynard Smith, *Evolution and the Theory of Games* (Cambridge:

something that occurs between relatives and that comes about because help given to relatives rebounds on the helper simply because relatives share the same genes: when a relative reproduces, one is, as it were, reproducing oneself by proxy. Another important mechanism (of which there are certainly strong intimations in Darwin's own writings) is "reciprocal altruism." This is where help is given on the "I'll scratch your back, if you scratch mine" principle.

As documented in Edward Wilson's magisterial *Sociobiology: The New Synthesis*, as well as in many, many subsequent works by him and others, we now have massive empirical evidence showing the workings of both kin selection and reciprocal altruism throughout the animal kingdom.[13] (There are even those who think one can see analogues in the plant kingdom.) Most important, it is abundantly clear that these mechanisms have and continue to operate among humans. When you think about it, this point is fairly obvious. Humans, in the last ten million years particularly, have gone the route of sociality. We are not particularly strong. We are not particularly fast. We are not particularly agile. At least, not when you compare us to other mammals, including those closest to us, the great apes. However, we are good at working together. Primitive humans were incredibly good hunters, because they learned how to work together. (In this respect we are much like wolves, and there are those students of animal behavior who suggest that wolves are in fact a much better model of human evolution than the great apes.)

At this point there is a very important fact to be noted. Many of the lower animals are entirely "genetically determined," meaning that what they do they do without thought because it is (as it were) imprinted on their genes. The social insects—ants, bees, wasps and others—are very efficient at working together, they are highly "altruistic," and obviously they do all of this without thinking about it at all. There are obviously great evolutionary advantages to this way of behaving. However, there

---

Cambridge University Press, 1982); George C. Williams, *Adaptation and Natural Selection* (Princeton, N.J.: Princeton University Press, 1966); Robert Trivers, "The Evolution of Reciprocal Altruism," *Quarterly Review of Biology* 46 (1971): 35-57.

[13]Edward O. Wilson, *Sociobiology: The New Synthesis* (Cambridge, Mass.: Harvard University Press, 1975).

are also evolutionary disadvantages. Most particularly, genetic determination means that if things change or go wrong, there is very little you can do to recoup your losses or alter direction. In the case of the social insects, this probably does not matter a great deal. The queen has literally hundreds of thousands of offspring. If she loses a few, say through predators or unfavorable environmental conditions, then so be it. There are plenty more. Higher animals like humans, however, do not have this luxury or option. We take a great deal of parental care to bring us to majority. Parents can rear at most a dozen offspring or so. Hence, we cannot afford to lose offspring capriciously, when faced with predators or bad weather or the like. We need evolutionary strategies to enable us to respond to change, to readjust and to go forward. In other words, we humans cannot be simply genetically determined.

Obviously, nature has tackled this problem by giving us large brains which enable us to work out ways of dealing with challenges. But note that in the case of a social species like *Homo sapiens,* our biggest challenges are almost always going to be those of dealing with our fellow humans. We have got to get on with each other, we've got to learn how to deal with difficult situations, and also we have to deal with enemies (whatever or whoever these may be, including fellow humans). What evolutionary biologists believe, therefore, is that nature has given our brains certain genetically determined, strategic rules or directives, which we then bring into play when dealing with new awkward situations. Rather like a self-correcting machine, let us say Mars Rover, which can adjust its direction and go around large rocks and so forth (without direction from Mother Earth), so we humans can adjust and go in different directions when faced with obstacles to our well being. The rules are fixed, but how we use the rules is not.[14]

It is at this point that morality comes into play. It is generally accepted by evolutionary biologists that some of these directives are moral norms. In other words we are genetically determined to believe that we ought to help each other. Note that crucially a sense of moral obligation comes into play here. It is not simply a matter of *wanting* to help each

---

[14]D. C. Dennett, *Elbow Room: The Varieties of Free Will Worth Wanting* (Cambridge, Mass.: MIT Press, 1984).

other, which sometimes we do want to do and sometimes we don't want to do. It is a question of feeling that we *ought* to help each other. This is somewhat stronger than simple emotion and gets us to cooperate and work together even when there might be a natural inclination not to do so. Note also that the genetic determination does not mean that we always will be moral. It is rather that we have the sense that we should be moral. (No one, other than perhaps the French existentialists at their most absurd, has ever seriously suggested that we choose the moral norms. The moral norms are imposed upon us, and it is a matter of whether or not we will obey them.)

Putting things together now, what I suggest is that the kind of general, normal feelings of substantive morality (that someone like me has) are very much what one would have expected to have emerged from the Darwinian evolutionary process. In other words, there is no reason to think either that I am kidding myself or, hypocritically, that I am trying to deceive you. There is nothing in Darwinism to suggest that truly I believe that we should all go out and rape and pillage, but that if it is in our interests to pretend otherwise, we will deny absolutely our innermost convictions.

Does this then mean that my Darwinian stance has no bite at all? Is there nothing in any of this that might lead one to pause for a moment and reconsider? I certainly think that this is a possibility. Humans are pretty good at deceiving themselves, and sometimes we do need to stop and ask ourselves whether we truly and genuinely believe what we say. I don't mean that we are particularly weak, but that this is the human condition. In the case of ethics, I have long been fascinated (well before I tried to put everything into a Darwinian context) by the gap between what we often say we should do and what we think we really should do. Go back to one of the basic moral claims that I instanced at the beginning of this section, about the differential obligations we have to family, friends and strangers. I think there are few of us who have not at one time or another been caught up with the claim that we owe help and friendship indifferently to all human beings. Indeed, those who were brought up as Christians know full well the parable of the good Samaritan.

And yet I wonder whether any of us really believe this. My strong suspicion is that most of us truly believe our first obligations are to our own children, and then to friends and their children, and only later to other members of our society, extending our range to peoples across the world. Put it this way: suppose you learned that instead of spending the bulk of my income on my family, I gave 90 percent to the Salvation Army or to Oxfam, meaning that my children had to eat at soup kitchens and could only wear hand-me-downs. In the summer the closest they get to a vacation is going out onto the street and opening up a fire hydrant. Would you think me a moral saint or a moral ogre? My suspicion is that most of us would opt for the second disjunct. This kind of emotion clearly fits well with evolutionary biology. Although reciprocal altruism suggests there are good reasons why you should not neglect the wants of strangers, pretty obviously kin selection dictates that family comes first, followed by friends and others in one's social circle—that is to say, people who are much more likely to come to your aid when you need help than would total strangers. So what I'm suggesting is that, with respect to substantive ethics, even some of the nuances of moral behavior fit nicely within a Darwinian evolutionary approach.

METAETHICS

Thus far I have been dealing with substantive or normative ethics, that is to say with questions about what one ought to do. What about the matter of foundations or justification? Let us start as before with traditional evolutionary ethics or Social Darwinism. The answer given here by everybody is unambiguous and straightforward. From Herbert Spencer to Edward O. Wilson, traditional evolutionary ethicists have seen the evolutionary process as progressive, going from the simple to the complex, from the worthless to the worthy, from (as they used to say in the nineteenth century) the monad to man.[15] We start with very primitive organisms, work up through fish, amphibians, reptiles, mammals and primates, and finally end up with *Homo sapiens*. This is obviously a good thing, and as such is the ultimate source of morality.

---

[15]Michael Ruse, *Monad to Man: The Concept of Progress in Evolutionary Biology* (Cambridge, Mass.: Harvard University Press, 1996).

Hence, we have the obligation to cherish the evolutionary process, helping it if we can and at the very least not standing in its way.

Therefore, if and when someone like Herbert Spencer argues for a *laissez-faire* view of society, he is not doing this because he is mean or unkind. He has nothing against the losers, widows and children, as such. It is just that he believes that *laissez-faire* will lead to upward rise, and ultimately this is a good thing for everyone. Likewise, when Alfred Russel Wallace promotes socialism and Prince Peter Kropotkin promotes anarchism, they too are arguing that this helps the evolutionary process, which is ultimately a good thing for everyone. Julian Huxley was not in favor of large-scale public works simply for their own sake, but because he thought that these would help the upward rise of humankind. It was he who insisted particularly that UNESCO include a science component, because he thought that it is exclusively through science that the human race will continue its upward rise. Finally, we find that Edward O. Wilson is a very enthusiastic progressionist, and in writing after writing he is explicit that he believes unless we promote biodiversity the human race will literally wither and die. A world of plastic would be totally destructive. We have evolved in symbiotic relationship with the rest of nature, and in order to ensure our continued existence, we must therefore ensure the continued existence of the rest of nature.[16]

As critics from both philosophy and biology have pointed out, there is something deeply flawed about this argument. Even before Darwin (and I should say that I don't really think that Darwin was a traditional evolutionary ethicist in this respect), there were those pointing out that there must be something fallacious about the kind of inference just presented. One is going from statements about the course of nature to statements about moral obligation. In other words, one is going from statements about matters of fact to statements about matters of morality. As David Hume pointed out in the eighteenth century, there is something illicit in this transition. Simply because something is the case, it does not follow that that something ought to be the case. At the

---

[16]Edward O. Wilson, *The Diversity of Life* (Cambridge, Mass.: Harvard University Press, 1992).

beginning of the twentieth century, the English philosopher G. E. Moore made a similar argument, pointing out that traditional evolutionary ethicists commit what he called the "naturalistic fallacy."[17] Trying to explain morality in terms of natural facts simply cannot be done.

Although he did not put the point in quite the same language, Darwin's supporter Thomas Henry Huxley made a similar critique. In his great essay "Evolution and Ethics," given in 1893, Huxley argued forcefully that the fact that things have evolved does not at all imply that they are good things.[18] The claws and teeth of the tiger are good for the tiger, but it does not follow at all that they are good generally. In fact, Huxley went as far as to say that, in his opinion, morality involves the very opposite from going with the course of evolution. Often morality means going against evolution. Evolution leads to strife and fighting and disharmony, and this is clearly no good thing. Morality therefore involves overcoming the evolved beast within each of us. As you might imagine from what I have said in the last section, I would not go as far as Huxley. I agree with him that in certain respects obviously we are selfish and violent. I would argue, however, that our friendliness and willingness to cooperate are likewise part of human nature and likewise the products of evolution. Overall, however, Huxley's point stands. Clearly there are some things that have evolved which by no means and by no stretch of the imagination would we regard as good. Hence, if we are going to cherry pick from the evolutionary process those things we think are good and discard those things we think are bad, we must be appealing to some higher or other foundation for morality.

NO FOUNDATIONS!

So let me make it absolutely clear: I am an ardent evolutionary ethicist. However, I reject absolutely the traditional justification offered by evolutionary ethicists, namely, the progressive nature of the evolutionary process. I am not sure whether in any meaningful sense one can talk about evolution as "progressive." Even if one can, though, I do not think

---

[17]G. E. Moore, *Principia Ethica* (Cambridge, Mass.: Cambridge University Press, 1903).

[18]Thomas Henry Huxley, *Evolution and Ethics with a New Introduction*, ed. Michael Ruse (Princeton, N.J.: Princeton University Press, 2009).

that this can be a progress which leads to increased moral value. As it happens, I value humans over (let us say) the AIDS virus, warthogs and even chimpanzees. But this valuation does not come from my understanding or acceptance of the Darwinian evolutionary process. Apart from anything else, the AIDS virus is more successful, from an evolutionary perspective, than the higher apes. My point simply is that whatever one means by "success" in this context, one can hardly mean "of greater moral worth."

So how then do I justify my substantive ethical beliefs? I claim simply that there is no justification! I think the substantive ethics, claims like "love your neighbor as yourself," are simply psychological beliefs put in place by natural selection in order to maintain and improve our reproductive fitness. There is nothing more to them than that. They have no ultimate backing. I am therefore what is known by philosophers as an "ethical skeptic."[19] Sometimes my position is known as "moral nihilism." Regardless of whatever term is used, I want to emphasize that my skepticism or nihilism is not about the *existence* of substantive ethics. It is about the *foundations* of substantive ethics. I am therefore a "moral nonrealist." (I am not, however, a "moral noncognitivist." This is a term which has often been applied to the emotive theory of ethics. It implies that, ultimately, ethical claims do not make sense. They are simply expressions of emotion. To the contrary, I believe that ethical claims make perfectly good sense. "You ought not kill" means simply that killing is wrong. That is perfectly meaningful. It is just that I do not believe that ethical claims have any justification.)

Am I simply claiming ethical skepticism without any argument, or do I claim that ethical skepticism follows from my beliefs about evolutionary biology? I argue the latter. My argument is simply the following. If the evolutionary process is nonprogressive in any meaningfully moral way, and I think this is so, then we could as easily have evolved a completely different moral system from that which we have. Instead of thinking that we ought to love our neighbors, we might well think that we should hate our neighbors. Indeed, something like this is perfectly

---

[19]J. L. Mackie, *Ethics* (Harmondsworth, U.K.: Penguin, 1977).

possible. I like to call it the "John Foster Dulles system of morality," so named after the Secretary of State under President Eisenhower in the 1950s. Dulles hated the Russians, and he realized that the Russians hated him, but he also recognized that he needed to get on with them. This he did very successfully, but without in any sense invoking what we would call traditional morality. He took their hate into account just as he took his own hate into account.

So what I'm suggesting is that we humans could as easily have evolved a completely different set of substantive moral norms. This poses a difficulty for those who want to claim that morality has some objective justification, that is to say the "moral realists." In fact, I would say that the difficulty is pretty close to an outright contradiction. At the least, one has to allow that if indeed there is a genuine morality backed by an objective foundation, it is perfectly possible that we have evolved in such a way as never to know it. And that, as I say, seems to me a very odd state of philosophical affairs. So, I do indeed want to claim that my moral nonrealism is not capricious but based on my beliefs about Darwinian evolutionary biology.

Incidentally, I do not accept as well-taken a counterargument based on mathematics. If you say that whether or not evolution is progressive, we are bound to accept $2 + 2 = 4$ and not $2 + 2 = 5$, I agree. I don't see how we could run our lives if we accepted the latter rather than the former. My whole point about the Dulles system of morality is that I think we could run our lives without accepting the particular moral system that we do accept. An analogous argument applies to claims about the necessity of sensing moving trains (if one is standing on the lines). I agree that there may be more than one way of sensing the train, but ultimately sense it you must. This is not so of our moral system. (Perhaps all systems of morality must conform to the same formal game-theoretic structure, meaning that there are formal rules of reciprocation that are needed for social living—like "always return a favor with a favor, but if not offered a favor refuse to reciprocate"—but as Kant knew well, it is filling in the details—that which goes beyond the formal—that counts.)[20]

---

[20]Immanuel Kant, *Foundations of the Metaphysics of Morals* (Indianapolis: Bobbs-Merrill, 1959).

Note that I am not now doing what I accuse the traditional evolutionary ethicists of mistakenly doing. I am not now justifying my substantive ethics. I'm not even justifying my substantive ethics in a kind of negative way by saying that it has no justification. I am rather explaining away the foundations of substantive ethics. If you like, I am doing an end run around the problems rather than trying to drive right through them. For this reason, far from ignoring Hume's dichotomy between "is" (matters of fact) and "ought" (matters of obligation), far from trying to break through it, far from saying that it is unimportant or irrelevant, I am strongly endorsing its truth. I argue that it is essential in understanding the nature of morality and its putative causes. I really do think that there is a big difference between saying something like "I don't want to kill a rival for the hand of my fiancée" and "it would be morally wrong for me to kill the rival for the hand of my fiancée." Part of the empirical case I would make for the evolution of morality is that the moral sense is something completely new, over and above normal feelings. It is, as I tried to point out earlier, something that can be used to enforce feelings and actions even when we are reluctant to do things. Like David Hume himself, I am a complete naturalist in matters of moral understanding. I think one can explain morality, but not justify it. However, I think that after one has given an explanation, one sees that calls for justification are out of place.

Let me make one final point about my position. You might now wonder, since I've agreed that substantive morality has no foundation, whether or not I'm opening the way for somebody simply to ignore moral norms. After all, they have no basis, so why bother to follow them? I think here we can get a lot of insight from Fyodor Dostoevsky's novel *Crime and Punishment.* There, the student Raskolnikov murdered an old woman for her money and thought that this was an end to matters because there is no objective morality. But, as Dostoevsky pointed out, matters were not quite that simple. Raskolnikov was a human being like the rest of us and as such had emotions and feelings of guilt. You will remember that in the novel the detective knew full well that Raskolnikov was guilty, but the latter was only charged and convicted after he himself had confessed. My point simply is that our psychology is very strong. We may know that morality has no objective foundation, but this does not mean that we can simply go out and ignore it.

I argue that an important part of what one might call the phenomenological experience of morality is that it is objective. When I say "killing is wrong," I don't just mean that I feel that killing is wrong. I mean that killing truly is absolutely, objectively wrong. That is why I believe it myself, but also why I think I have the right and obligation to say this to you. I'm not just telling you about my own emotions or feelings, I'm telling you what I think holds for us all. Note the important qualification that I am speaking at what I have just called the "phenomenological" level. If I am right philosophically, then there is no absolute, objective basis to morality. I am talking about how we feel and what we mean. In other words, I am talking about our psychology, if you like. My position is exactly that of David Hume when he claimed that his philosophical inquiries led him to skepticism, but that after a while back in the real world (playing backgammon and so forth) his psychology took over and he didn't bother about the skepticism.

Just as for Hume and his skepticism about the world, there are obvious Darwinian reasons why we should thus "objectivize" morality. If we knew that morality was subjective and that we could ignore it, then very quickly morality would break down and people would start cheating and before long there would be general mayhem. But because we think that morality is objective, we all obey it more or less. In other words, I'm saying it is a Darwinian adaptation that we should be deceived about the justificatory status of morality. Morality may have no foundation, but it is in our biological interests that we should think that it has. Hence we do think that it has.

NATURAL LAW THEORY

Having now explained my own position on morality, both substantive ethics and metaethics, I want to bring this discussion to a close by relating my thinking to the thinking of religious people, specifically to the thinking of Christians. I have long argued that science and religion are going to clash if one holds to some of the literalist beliefs dear to American fundamentalists (today, better known as creationists). One cannot accept Darwinian evolution or indeed modern cosmology and at the same time accept a six-thousand-year, six-day story of creation.[21] However, in line with more sophisticated (and traditional) Christians, I have always also argued that it is open to the believer to interpret the Bible metaphorically or allegorically when it clashes with modern science. Hence, I see no basic reason why one should not be both an enthusiast for modern science and a practicing Christian. In particular, I see no reason why one should not accept Darwinian evolutionary theory and the basic claims of the Christian faith—Creator God, humans made in God's image, original sin, incarnation and atonement, possibility of salvation and eternal life.

I have written much elsewhere on this general problem and will not therefore repeat myself here.[22] Instead, I will focus on the issue of morality. Surely, you might with reason think the theory of morality I have presented thus far in this essay clashes completely and absolutely with Christian thinking on the matter of ethical behavior and justification. If Christianity stands for anything, it stands for an absolute morality (meaning morality at the substantive level), backed for justification by the existence and desires of the Creator God. I, to the contrary, have argued that ultimately morality is a matter of psychology, without foundation. In words that seem to have become somewhat notorious in certain circles, I have claimed that morality is "an illusion put in place by our genes to make us social facilitators."[23] You cannot get much further from Christianity than this. Hence, despite any warm and friendly feelings I might have toward Christians, I hold beliefs that if well taken show Christianity to be false.

I deny completely that this follows. The system of morality I have presented is one based completely and absolutely on methodological naturalistic thinking, and says nothing at all about metaphysical naturalism. By this I mean the position I have presented is one that takes no

---

[21]Robert T. Pennock and Michael Ruse, eds., *But Is It Science? The Philosophical Question in the Creation/Evolution Controversy*, 2nd ed. (Buffalo, N.Y.: Prometheus, 2008).

[22]See Ruse, *Can a Darwinian Be a Christian?*; *Evolution-Creation Struggle*; and *Science and Spirituality*.

[23]Michael Ruse and E. O. Wilson, "The Evolution of Morality," *New Scientist* 1478 (1985): 108-28.

account whatsoever of God. If you like, I am a methodological atheist, but at the same time make no claims whatsoever about the existence or nonexistence of God. If you like, I am a metaphysical agnostic. In other words, I believe that one could be a metaphysical theist if one so wished. I don't want to be a metaphysical theist, and I think you are wrong if you are a metaphysical theist, but that is a different matter. I don't argue against you on this score using science as a weapon but rather philosophically and theologically, for instance raising the problem of evil.

How can I make the case for the compatibility of my moral thinking with Christian belief? I start by pointing out that, at the substantive level, I don't think there's really any difference between me and the Christian. It is well known that Christians, even liberal Christians, tend to be all over the place with respect to particular moral norms. But as I tried to point out earlier, I think of these differences less as matters of ultimate morality and more as interpretation and difference about matters of fact and of the relevance of these matters of fact to moral decision making. One Christian, for instance, might be in favor of gay marriage, whereas another might be against it. But I don't think that either differs ultimately about morality. The differences, rather, are about the nature of sexual orientation, the implications of various practices for society as a whole, and much more. I take it that ultimately Christians believe that one should follow the love commandment, that is to say, treating one's neighbors as oneself. I accept this completely. The big issues are what it means to say someone is one's neighbor and what it means to say that one is treating somebody as one would treat oneself.

So, allowing that there is a lot of hard work to be done, I repeat that at the substantive level I see little difference between myself and the Christian. Nor am I impressed by objections. First, you might argue the parable of the good Samaritan implies that the Christian does have equal obligations to everyone, whereas I have denied this. But even here matters are not entirely clear. Certainly, Saint Paul thought that we have special obligations to family and others close to us—and note that I have not denied there is a place for being a good Samaritan. It is just that I think "charity begins at home." And this many Christians would accept also. Second, do not accuse me of relativism, arguing that no Christian could accept the moral variation to which I am committed. I am a subjectivist, not a relativist. I argue that certain adaptations do not work unless they are fairly standard and shared by the group. There is little point in my speaking beautiful English if you all speak a dialect and you cannot follow me and I cannot follow you. Language has to be standardized. The same is true of morality. If our moralities differ at the basic level, then dialogue and sociality break down. I reject relativism.[24]

It is the metaethical level where we seem to have problems and differences. I want to argue that there is no justification on this level. The Christian wants to argue that there is and that this justification ultimately goes back to God. Note at once two things. First, as I've just explained, I am a methodological atheist. So, speaking as a methodological atheist, I think there is no justification. However, if one opens the scope of debate and allows for the existence of God, I see no reason why my position bars God being involved at some level in the matter of justification. It is just that, speaking as a naturalist, I see no justification. I admit that as a naturalist I am quite happy with my position and feel no need for anything further. But we knew that all along. The Christian as Christian does feel the need for something further, and the question really is whether the Christian can add on something to my position without getting into contradiction.

The second thing to be noted is that Christians have reason to tread very carefully when they appeal to God to justify morality (that is to say, to justify substantive morality). There is the well-known Euthyphro problem. Does God want us to do that which is good simply because it is the will of God? Or is there some other standard, beyond God, to which he and we must subscribe? In other words, could God make rape and pillage morally acceptable? If he could, then he really doesn't seem

---

[24]Do I think that we could have relativism across societies and cultures? In some respects obviously, if only because different societies and cultures have different factual beliefs. People like Darwin and Huxley genuinely thought that women should not go to university because their brains are not up to it. Whenever they menstruate, their thinking powers collapse. We know better now and, to prove it, women are by far the majority at universities in the West. But especially given that humans all came from one small population about 150,000 years ago, I see no reason to think that basically we have different moral codes.

to be the kind of good God that we hold to and want to worship. If he couldn't, then it seems that there is some standard of morality external to God.

The usual way—and in my opinion, by far the best and most sophisticated way—around this problem is to adopt some version of St. Thomas Aquinas's "natural law theory." Here one argues that morality comes out of what is natural.[25] God has created human beings in certain ways in order that we can function and enjoy life fully. Being moral is behaving according to these natural functions. Thus, for instance, having and rearing children is a morally good thing because human beings are fitted to have and rear children. Conversely, deliberately harming yourself, just for kicks, is morally wrong because you are interfering with natural function. (Of course, the sophisticated natural law theorist is aware that sometimes people do things because they are sick rather than because they are moral. I accept these reservations as if they were already articulated.) Thus, natural law theory sees that morality is not just arbitrary, but at the same time it sees morality as something that stems from God and his goodness. God is not capricious. God made us the way that we are in order to function and to enjoy things fully. But, as a consequence of this, there are actions which follow naturally, and these are things that we ought to do.

Again, anticipating objections, I accept fully that there's going to be considerable debate about what is natural or nonnatural in a particular circumstance. For instance, Roman Catholics believe that contraception is unnatural. My contrary suspicion is that the natural law theorist today could well point to the fact that sexual intercourse between humans has functions over and above their reproduction. It helps to promote pair bonding, which is something extremely important in the raising of children. Given the way that, thanks to modern medicine, we have interfered artificially with the number of children that a couple might now expect to have (jacking the number up significantly) and yet have not really changed the number we might reasonably be expected to raise, one could readily argue that spacing a family using contracep-

---

[25]Philip L. Quinn, *Divine Commands and Moral Requirements* (Oxford: Clarendon, 1978).

tion is very much a natural thing to do, and hence is morally obligated under natural law theory.

Suppose for the sake of argument one accepts natural law theory. We have an almost perfect fit between theology and scientifically informed philosophy. As a Christian, doing what is natural is doing what is moral. As a Darwinian, doing what is natural is doing what is moral. In other words, we agree entirely! The Christian says that loving your neighbor as yourself is right because the feeling that one should love one's neighbor as oneself is something built into human nature by God, and that is all there is to things. The Darwinian says loving your neighbor as yourself is right because the feeling that one should love one's neighbor as oneself is something built into human nature by natural selection, and that is all there is to things. The two claims mesh perfectly together.

Let me repeat and tackle again what I think will be the main point of difficulty for some. I argue, as a naturalist, there is no need to go further than the scientific-cum-philosophical explanation. The Christian argues that, as a theist, there is need to go further than the scientific-cum-philosophical explanation. The Christian therefore adds God into the equation. But note that adding God into the equation is, as both naturalist and Christian will agree, to go beyond naturalism. The Christian argues that only by going beyond naturalism does one get the full context. This is something that we can debate, but note that the debate is not a scientific debate. It is more one of philosophy or theology. It has nothing to do with Darwinian evolution or any other scientific theory, as such. So while I fully agree that there might be differences between believers and nonbelievers—surely a fact that we already knew—I maintain my position that there need be no difference over the theory of morality that I have offered. Or rather, any difference is over whether or not my position is complete. I am satisfied with what I said. The Christian is not. But the Christian's dissatisfaction is not with the content of what I said, but with its scope. The Christian can, and I believe should, accept fully what I have said about morality. He or she can then add on something more. I don't think we need something more, but that is another matter.

CONCLUSION

In conclusion, let me say that I am always worried about new philosophical theories. Alfred North Whitehead used to say that either they are wrong or they are in Plato already. I'm not sure that my position can be found in Plato. However, as I've already intimated, I do think that I am writing very much in the spirit of David Hume. Hume was not an evolutionist, so I'm certainly going beyond his thinking. I am adding in the science of the nineteenth century, but in essence the very last thing I am arguing is that my position is all that radical. I recognize that traditionally Hume's philosophy has been taken to be something in opposition to Christianity, and there is obviously good reason for this assumption. But the particular part I am appropriating is not necessarily opposed to all religious thought. Thomas Aquinas was a naturalist because he drew heavily on Aristotle, who was no less a naturalist than Hume. Therefore let me conclude by saying that I think we naturalists should stick together, and it is in this conciliatory spirit that I end this essay.

A Naturalist Moral Realism Response

Evan Fales

MICHAEL RUSE AND I ARE BOTH NATURALISTS. We share the belief that there are no gods (though I am perhaps a bit more confident of that than Ruse); a fortiori, we both deny that God had anything to do with the presence of *Homo sapiens* on planet Earth. We both consider the existence of our species to be a cosmic happenstance—a development brought about by an uncountable myriad of natural accidents, coupled with the processes of biological reproduction and natural selection. We are, that is, both stout neo-Darwinians. But I am a moral realist and Ruse is not. Whence the difference?

The keys to our disagreement are, I think, two. My diagnosis is that Ruse sees in the vagaries and lack of "purpose" or "progress" in evolutionary processes no room for a foundation for morality, whereas I find there precisely the basis for such a foundation, and, even more fundamentally, that Ruse has been seduced by a quasi-religious conception of (realist) morality as something that requires grounding or justification in some reality that stands apart from the lived realities of sentient beings—and so is able to pass judgment upon them (whereas I deny this). Let me explain.

Ruse draws a distinction, as is standard, between normative ethics and metaethics. Let us grant it. With respect to our normative ethical convictions, he has something rather surprising to say:

> If the evolutionary process is nonprogressive in any meaningfully moral way, . . . then we could as easily have evolved a completely different moral system from that which we have. . . .
>
> At the least, one has to allow that if indeed there is a genuine morality backed by an objective foundation, it is perfectly possible that we have evolved in such a way as never to know it. (pp. 65-66)

Here we have two claims, one empirical, the other, drawn from it, epistemological. The first claim is ambiguous. Does Ruse mean to be claiming that we, as we are but prescinding from our moral instincts, intuitions and beliefs (that is, with the same nonmoral cognitive, affective and physiological nature) could have "easily evolved" a different moral system, or is he claiming that "we" might have easily evolved as creatures with significantly different natures and a correspondingly different moral system? On the second reading, the claim is perhaps true, but in this context uninteresting. (It is notoriously hard to evaluate such counterfactual claims: are we to allow that proto-humans might easily have encountered very different adaptive conditions and so evolved differently, or are we to suppose that they might easily have evolved differently under the same adaptive conditions?)

On its first interpretation, I should be strongly inclined to deny the first claim. Are we to suppose that, being the creatures we essentially are (i.e., fundamentally rational, social creatures with the ability to reflect upon our nature, with long-term pair bonding as a major resource in the successful rearing of children, etc.) we might have "easily" developed a moral system in which, say, there was no institution of marriage and no obligation to be faithful to one's spouse(s), in which "Commit murder whenever you get badly irritated" was *de rigueur*, in which lying and stealing were considered morally irrelevant, and (as in Butler's *Erewhon*), illness was morally reprehensible? I think not. It is no accident that our moral systems reflect those practices essential to our well-being.[1]

Nor is the second claim plausible—unless one thought that normative moral principles have nothing essentially to do with what sorts of beings we are and what sorts of things enable us to flourish. This brings me to my second point. Ruse observes that "Huxley argued forcefully that the fact that things have evolved does not at all imply that they are good things. The claws and teeth of the tiger are *good for the tiger*, but it does not follow that they are good generally" (p. 64, emphasis added.)

Now I have no idea what it means for something to be good "generally," but I suspect that notion, if it has any content at all, derives from the vaguely theological idea that there are such things as "cosmic" goods.

---

[1]Ruse may actually agree: elsewhere he says, "the kind of general, normal feelings of substantive morality . . . are very much what one would have expected to have emerged from the Darwinian evolutionary process" (p. 61). So I am not sure how to take Ruse's first claim.

At any rate, Ruse himself allows that there are such things as things good for tigers, and that's the only sort of good that I think we need to give moral realism a foundation. Teeth and claws are good things for a tiger (if not for the prey); pain and suffering are bad. So, other things being equal, it is wrong—objectively wrong—to torment a tiger.[2] Tigers—sentient creatures generally—are morally consideration worthy. Why should one think that objective evils could only consist in something like storming the gates of heaven or "harming" the cosmos? But if that is not what Ruse means by "general evil/good," then I have no grip on what is meant. That sentient creatures have the natures they have is an objective fact; thus I claim that principles of conduct toward such creatures derived from facts about their natures are objective. That is the only sensible standard for the moral realist to meet.

At the heart of Ruse's thinking, of course, is Hume's dictum that one can't derive an "ought" from an "is." To do so is to commit a naturalistic fallacy. I reject Hume's dictum. Of course I agree that there is no *formal* entailment relation that runs from "is" to "ought." For one thing, many "is" statements bear no necessary connection to "oughts" at all. It is only certain facts about teleologically organized systems that carry such a normative burden. But even here the relation is certainly not one of formal entailment. Rather, it is a relation of conceptual or metaphysical necessity. More precisely, I should say that the following is a fair reconstruction. Teleological facts about teleological systems are related to nonteleological facts about them by way of metaphysical necessity (perhaps by way of a supervenience relation). Given certain nonteleological facts, teleological facts follow as a matter of metaphysical necessity. That those teleological facts, in turn, "entail" ought statements is a matter of *conceptual* necessity. It is a conceptual truth, given certain teleological facts about x, that certain things are good for x, either intrinsically or instrumentally. And it is conceptually necessary that certain "oughts" follow from the facts about what is good for x.

---

[2] You might think that pain and suffering are bad for any creature capable of experiencing them, so bad *tout court*. Perhaps. But I understand that morphine, rather than deadening pain, makes one indifferent to it. If so, there could be creatures with brains so constructed that the experience of pain is not, per se, a bad for them.

I am unsure how exactly to understand Ruse's psychologizing of morality. This is rather important for whether his effort to achieve a détente with theistic metaethical theories can succeed. Near as I can tell, Ruse readily agrees that all normal human beings—including, of course, himself—share certain moral sentiments. But these moral feelings are not indicators of or evidence for any objective rights and wrongs. They are nothing more than the subjective deposits of evolutionary processes. Thus (to illustrate), Ruse sees in Raskolnikov's inability to maintain his defense against the canny probing of police inspector Porfiry Petrovich nothing more than the fateful operation of certain mental mechanisms: "our psychology is very strong."

I—and I think also theists—will see Raskolnikov's situation very differently. It's not that Ruse is mistaken about the strength of "psychology," but that, in seeing Raskolnikov as the unhappy victim of the self-recriminations of his own psychology, Ruse has possibly missed a much deeper theme in Dostoyevsky's portrait of his protagonist. Raskolnikov is a saint—though a saint whose soul has become deeply led astray, enmeshed in the seductions of a destructive intellectual sickness. Yet we are left with hope: the hope that his soul will be fully restored through the sacrifices of another saint, his guardian angel Sonya.

What do I mean in saying that Raskolnikov is a saint? I mean, among other things, that in his innermost being he is (and always was) instinctively driven by an orientation toward the good, and that this orientation does not—or does not *merely*—consist in a set of feelings or emotional responses but also in an ultimate recognition that, his Enlightenment moral "theories" to the contrary notwithstanding, his act of murder is, really and in fact, a terrible sin.[3] Even in the crucible in which his better nature finally triumphs over his justification for the murder, the question he faces is never which of his feelings will win the day but whether what he has done is permissible.

Is Ruse then able to achieve a kind of rapprochement with Christian theists over moral theory, as he claims? Matters are not, I suggest, very straightforward. First, though, a rather local matter on which I would

---

[3]I don't think this nearly does justice to the notion of sainthood for Dostoyevsky. But this isn't the place for that discussion.

be inclined to support Ruse. Does the parable of the good Samaritan commit Christians to the principle of an equal regard for all human beings? Is it an expression of a kind of moral universalism? How we should understand the import of the parable needs to be sensitive to the historical and cultural context in which it was composed.

As is well known, the Samaritans were a Jewish sect that broke with the Jerusalem-centered Judean strain of Judaism, with its cultus centered at another Jewish holy site, Mount Gerizim (in opposition to the temple on Mount Zion).[4] Mutual hostility over which group constituted the "true" Jews and keepers of Yahweh's covenant abounded. Clearly Jesus' parable about who is one's neighbor means to elide that boundary, and it can be argued that it is a microcosm of a much larger redrawing of the boundaries that is implicit in the teachings of Jesus: an expansion of the boundaries of the land of the Promise from Judea to the Roman Empire. But whether any true universalism is implied, as opposed to a politically courageous response to Roman hegemony is, I think, a very open question.

To turn now to the general question. For the purposes of rapprochement, Ruse insists that his position is committed only to methodological atheism, not to metaphysical atheism. This in itself cannot be squared with what Ruse calls his moral nihilism: with the claim that there is no justification for his substantive (i.e., normative) ethical beliefs. But Ruse allows that though speaking as a naturalist he sees no justification for moral norms, he is willing to entertain the supposition that there is a God and to consider how things might go then. His strategy is to suggest that a theist who embraces a theistic natural-law metaethical theory can cleanly graft his theistic metaethics onto Ruse's Darwinian view of normative ethics.

But I doubt this, or at least I'm not sure how it's supposed to go. The general idea is that God will have made us (via Darwinian processes, I suppose: Ruse isn't going to jettison that—or is he?) so that, if we do what comes naturally to us, we will "enjoy things fully." What comes naturally to us is determined, so Ruse would have it, *inter alia* by the

---

[4]Tellingly, the Samaritans identified Gerizim with Mount Moriah—the mountain on which Abraham nearly sacrificed Isaac—whereas the Judahite Jews identified Moriah with Zion.

instincts and moral feelings that we find ourselves with. I have two questions right away. What does "enjoying things fully" amount to? Is this another phrase for what Aristotle meant by *eudaimonia*? Or is it perhaps to be understood hedonistically? And what moral role, if any beyond the calculation of means-ends relations, does Ruse envision for rational reflection? Both these questions, which are far too large to pursue further here, reflect what I think will be a central concern for the theist, namely, whether Ruse's account of morality, and indeed of the nature of our moral feelings, is adequate even at the normative level. At least to this extent: for Ruse, any sense we have that our moral sensibilities reflect objective realities—as surely we do have—are illusory, whereas for the natural-law theorist, they are very far from being so. Theists are also likely to disagree with Ruse over what the ultimate aims of human life are and over what obligations derive from those aims. But here, perhaps it would be better to let the theist parties to this conversation have the final say.

A Moral Essentialism Response

Keith E. Yandell

> We need evolutionary strategies to enable us to respond to change, to readjust and to go forward. . . . [W]e humans cannot be simply genetically determined. . . .
>
> The rules are fixed, but how we use the rules is not. . . .
>
> Part of the empirical case I would make for the evolution of morality is that the moral sense is something completely new, over and above normal feelings. . . .
>
> Morality is a matter of psychology, without foundation. . . .
>
> If we knew that morality was subjective and that we could ignore it, then very quickly morality would break down and . . . before long there would be general mayhem. But because we think that morality is objective, we all obey it more or less. . . . [I]t is a Darwinian adaptation that we be deceived about the justificatory status of morality.—Michael Ruse (pp. 60, 67, 69, 68)

INTRODUCTION

The first three quotations in the epigraph could be written by a theist without being inconsistent with his or her position. There is nothing contradictory to theism in thinking that morality evolves, if this means that only when there were persons to which it applied was it realized that there is a morality to obey. A moral sense is a distinct sense—both a recognition of what is right and some motivation toward doing it, what Kant called a "rational emotion." Further, persons are "not simply genetically determined" and various ways of action are open to them; they possess significant freedom. One can go on: God has brought about moral agents with a sense of right and wrong and an ability to act in ways other than the ones in which they do act.

Unfortunately Ruse makes the further claim that morality is (simply) a matter of psychology, a Darwinian adaptation, and our moral sense is a deception fortunate for survival. What we call morality, he says, is caused by tendencies to behave and a feeling unique to persons. Both have neo-Darwinian explanations. There are no obligations, only *feelings* of obligation. Such feelings have no more relation to reality than a strong sense of our being surrounded by unicorns.

NATURALIST MORAL NONREALISM

By his own account, Professor Ruse's view of morality is (A) nonsubjectivist—that something is good does not just mean that people like or approve of it; (B) nonrelativist—what is good does not vary from person to person or group to group; (C) nonemotivist—sentences like "Killing infants is wrong" does not translate into sentences like "Killing infants—UGH," which is neither true nor false; (D) nonrealist—there are no moral properties and no nonempirical moral truths; (E) naturalist—there is no God, no immaterial soul (or anything else immaterial), and what makes moral statements true are facts accessible to empirical observation; and (F) substantive—as contrasted with metaethics, which deals with what, if anything, justifies claims in substantive ethics. Ruse holds that substantive ethics exhausts ethics; there is no metaethics, and this is no loss. (Note the different uses of *subjective* in the fifth quotation of the epigraph, where it means "without justification," and the adjectival form in (A) where it means "private to an individual.")

Ruse's naturalist moral nonrealism tells us that in the course of evolution we have developed various propensities to behave in certain ways. Which ways these are has been largely determined by their value for survival. We often act in accord with these tendencies, though they can be overcome by strong feelings and other propensities. These tendencies, and our acting from them, neither have nor need justification any more than a squirrel needs justification for eating acorns. The degree to which we deliberately act for survival preserving is not the point. The point is that those who are cooperators are better adapted to their environment and hence are "selected for," where this just means that they survive. The same holds for other morally positive actions and practices.

ETHICS AND REALISM VERSUS ANTIREALISM

Ruse's approach is quite different from moral realist views. A Kantian claims that "You ought always to so act as to show respect for other persons" is a fundamental principle of morality, and a Benthamite will offer "Always so act as to bring about the greatest balance of pleasure over pain, considering all those affected and the long run." No justification of these claims can involve deriving these principles from moral principles still deeper—there are none. For Kant, persons have "dignity, not price" and are "ends in themselves" (have intrinsic worth), and these are (informally) necessary truths. For a Benthamite, there is inherent value in pleasurable states. But a Rusean can make no appeal to intrinsic or inherent value. The discourse of his theory remains entirely descriptive. No "is-ought" gap here—the claims are descriptive, not normative. Thus for Ruse there is only the groundless *feeling* of obligation without any corresponding reality.

EVOLUTION AND ETHICS

Ruse explains our being attracted by cooperation and not by mass murder by reference to a strong feeling of obligation that has developed in the evolutionary process. This is not due to any relation to anything transcendent of natural properties, nor is there any obligation to any transcendent being (there being nothing transcendent to which to be obligated). Ruse's theory entails that the Kantian idea of morality as universal—as applying to all rational creatures of whatever sort because they are rational—is in error. The point here is more subtle than it may seem. For both Ruse and Kant, were we to live in an environment in which we survived only if decapitated and sewn back together once a day, then moral hesitations concerning decapitation would be needless and decapitation service would be a noble profession. What will harm someone will vary as we go from one sort of embodiment to another and one environment to another. Accordingly, so will what counts as respect. Kant's idea is that so long as one is dealing with a rational agent, one owes respect to this person since he or she has "dignity, not price." Ruse's idea is that we will behave as our evolutionary history has produced us to behave—namely, in accord with certain behavioral propensities. In bumper-sticker style: "Is is all, and ought is nought."

So, according to Ruse there aren't any obligations. There are just strong positive feelings, of a kind unique to our species, that motivate us to act. According to Ruse we have this experience and believe that we have obligations, and this makes us "social facilitators." Morality is an illusion necessary for the survival of the race. Had the path of evolution been different, we might have had different propensities. If we had, then the content of our morality would have been different. As it is, we exhibit plenty of noncooperative behavior and propensities unfavorable to survival. Had we enough more unfavorable-to-survival propensities, we might very well not have survived. This would have been no better or worse than our existing. Being good is simply typically acting in accord with a set of propensities that we have evolved to have, and acting in a manner that is good is simply acting in accord with those propensities, which play only a causal and explanatory role. There is no—indeed, cannot be any—appeal to the value of human persons on Ruse's view.

ETHICS WITHOUT THEISM

Ruse objects to there being any theistic basis for ethics. For Ruse, ethics needs no basis other than the *de facto* results of evolutionary processes. I take it these processes do not "aim at survival." Rather, as the environment changes, some creatures change in ways that accord with the new direction, others do not move with the times, and the latter pass from the scene. No transcendent basis for ethics of any sort is available or required. One set of mores is replaced by another, and we are still without an ethic.

EXPLAIN, NOT JUSTIFY

Ruse's purpose is to explain substantive morality. He views neo-Darwinism as enough to explain morality, and it uses no value terms in its scientifically proper formulation (whatever metaphors are used to present it to the public in a way that will make them feel better: Mother Nature, evolutionary intentions, progress to a higher stage of civilization, etc.). The fact is that survivors have adapted well enough to survive, and the behavior patterns that have made this possible are exhibited in what they find obligatory. This will remain the case until and unless the environment changes so that new behavior patterns are needed. Should this happen, things will be no better or worse than they are now. *Better* and *worse*, insofar as they have any sense, are relative to the propensities built into the survivors. If the propensities lead to murder and rape, then our mores will come to favor these, and in no objective sense will this be any worse than if the propensities led to love and peace.

SUBSTANTIVE ETHICS AND METAETHICS

As Ruse notes, the distinction between substantive ethics and metaethics is taken largely for granted in philosophy, but this does not play quite the role that Ruse suggests. Substantive ethical theories contain various elements; as full-blown theories they endeavor to answer various questions such as:

1. What makes something (a person or a state of affairs) good or bad? (In ethics, there are three possibilities: good, bad, neutral, so "not good" does not entail "bad" and "not bad" does not entail "good.")

2. What makes an action right or wrong?

3. Is goodness basic to rightness, or rightness basic to goodness, or are both basic?

4. What sort of life is worth living?

Metaethics concerns assessment of answers to these questions: what properties must a good answer have, and which if any of the proffered answers has these properties? On this account there are theories that answer questions one through four (and similar ones) and theories about how to assess answers. On Ruse's view, there really is no metaethics; he is clear about this and has no regrets.

My next suggestion is more controversial: Ruse has no substantive ethics. On his view there is just the fact that people have certain propensities to act and a distinct sort of strong feeling favoring some ways of acting. This is not a view in substantive ethics. There is no more substantive ethics on a Rusean view than there is metaethics. There are just neo-Darwinian claims about propensities and feelings.

Put differently, he offers a theory of *mores*—of behavioral rules and practices which people have adopted. He endeavors to give an evolutionary (biological) account of how these rules and practices arose. What he explains, anthropologists also describe: empirically discoverable rules that one finds in the cultures they study. Anthropologists study mores, not ethics. Ethics is inherently a normative discipline, trading in goodness, badness, rightness, wrongness and the like. To reduce it to a purely descriptive discipline is to *replace* it, not to explain it.

It seems to me that an accurate way of putting things from a Rusean perspective is something along the following lines: we have long thought that such terms as *intrinsic worth* and *value for its own sake* refer to properties that exist mind-independently. We have sought basic moral principles that provide the foundation of ethics and asked what sort of metaphysic can underlie and justify such principles. This has all been a sad error. Ethics has no metaphysical grounding. There are no fundamental moral principles accessible to reason or provided by revelation. There are simply empirical generalizations concerning our propensities and feelings, and concerning our mores and conduct. The whole story is descriptive, empirical and scientific. *Pace* Ruse, however, there is no philosophically substantive difference between his account of ethics and that of my anthropology professor who denied that there was anything more to so-called ethics than mores. The anthropologist observes mores and Ruse explains them. Neither is doing substantive ethics.

This feature of Ruse's view comes out in another way. Suppose the course of evolution had gone otherwise relative to the propensities produced in us. Suppose that our survival relevant propensities were cast differently so that dark-skinned people were anathema to light-skinned people but not conversely, and that light-skinned people happened to discover weapons of mass destruction first and used them to "neutralize" the dark-skinned population. Or suppose the reverse had been true. Would the former, or the latter, "population neutralization" have been bad, even evil? Not on naturalist moral nonrealism. It would simply be the case that what occurred did so because of propensities evolved from neo-Darwinian causes. There are no Rusean grounds to say otherwise, because rightness and wrongness are mores relative, and mores are propensity relative. The most Ruse could say is that either "neutralization" would be bad *given our current mores*, and under the new mores whether one or the other was good would likely depend on who neutralized whom.

I am not claiming, and I am confident it is false, that Ruse would approve of either change. That is not the point. The point is that on Ruse's theory *under the changed course of evolution described earlier*, the consistent answer is that neither "population neutralization" would be better or worse than their absence on any mores-independent grounds. Nor is one set of mores ethically superior to another, however different they may be relative to survival.

On Ruse's view, there just aren't any ethics; instead there are facts about how people behave and theories about why they behave that way. The facts are discerned by empirical observation. The theories to be taken most seriously are biological (and psychological). Nothing further is relevant.

Looking at things from another perspective: if our "morality" has no other source than our *de facto* propensities and a deceptive strong feeling, and morality would be different had they been different, why not make them different? No proposal is made to the effect that human persons have any intrinsic worth, so such considerations are not possible barriers to a revision of "morality"—strictly, of mores—that would, by present standards, be utterly immoral. If someone has the power to do this and can decide to use that power, what in Ruse's perspective could be a barrier to her doing so?

ANALYSIS OR REPLACEMENT?

Philosophers often disagree on how to describe a given attempt at reduction. Bishop Berkeley held that what we refer to as physical (mind-independent, spatially located) objects are really nothing more than ideas. Is this an analysis of the nature of physical objects or a claim that reference to physical objects is really reference to nonphysical items? I opt for the latter: conscious states, on Berkeley's view, are necessarily mind dependent and unlocated in space, and they are things that really exist. Similarly, whereas (I take it) Ruse proposes an explanation of substantive ethics, the explanation is also (or comes with) an account of what is being explained. I propose that this is a replacement. All that is left after his analysis is people's propensities to act in certain ways and feelings that certain things should be done or not done, with the illusion that there is something more involved than sheer feeling. A world of which this were true would be a world in which ethics is absent. Ruse might reply that what I call "all that is left" is really all there ever was. I disagree, but that is another topic. If there really ever was what Ruse allows, then there have never been anything more than mores.

APPENDIX

It is interesting that Ruse holds that human behavior is not determined lest we be unable to adopt survival strategies, and that a sense of obligation is unique to human persons. He, of course, sets these facts in a different context than would a theist. Many theists will see freedom of choice to be a condition of moral responsibility and hold that, while not infallible, a sense of obligation often connects us to ways in which we really ought to behave.

A Moral Particularism Response

Mark D. Linville

I HAVE LEARNED A GREAT DEAL FROM Professor Ruse's writings over the years, and I am honored to engage his ideas here.

Michael Ruse is a self-described ethical skeptic and moral nihilist. But we might take heart in the realization that, nihilist though he may be, he is a nice nihilist.[1] As he assures us, he shares the moral beliefs of the next fellow. I'm encouraged to learn of his love of family, fondness for babies and kind assistance to elderly grandmothers at crosswalks. I envision him engaged in arboreal rescue missions to retrieve frightened felines from dizzying heights and place them in the arms of anxious children. I'm certain that he agrees that "it is better to be truthful and good than to not."[2]

In what sense, then, is he a nihilist? On Professor Ruse's view, even our most deep-seated moral convictions "are simply psychological beliefs put in place by natural selection in order to maintain and improve our reproductive fitness" (p. 65). We believe and behave as we do not because there is any truth to the beliefs or because we have any objective duties so to behave. Rather, the beliefs prompt and reinforce behaviors that are—or were—adaptive from an evolutionary point of view.

According to Darwin, human morality is rooted in a set of social instincts that conferred reproductive fitness upon our ancestors given the circumstances of the evolutionary landscape. Some behaviors (feeding one's babies, fleeing from large predators) are adaptive, and others (feeding one's babies to large predators) are not. Any predisposition or prompting that increases the probability of the adaptive behavior will thus also be adaptive. The circumstances of early hominid evolution were such that various forms of altruistic behavior were fitness confer-

---

[1]According to Tamler Sommers and Alex Rosenburg, a "nice nihilist" believes that there are no moral facts but, like most everyone, is wired to behave as though there are. See their "Darwin's Nihilistic Idea: Evolution and the Meaninglessness of Life," *Biology and Philosophy* 18 (2003): 653-68.
[2]This classic understatement is a line from Steve Martin's character, a two-bit con artist named Freddy Benson, in the film *Dirty Rotten Scoundrels*.

ring. For instance, members of a cooperative and cohesive group would tend to have greater reproductive success since the group itself would tend to fare better than competing, discordant groups. Assuming that the cooperation is due at least in part to genetically derived predispositions, natural selection sets to work.

Such an evolutionary explanation for human morality explains the presence of human moral beliefs, but the explanation does not appear to require their being *true*. We believe as we do because the resulting behavior is—or was—fitness conferring. But (so it can be argued) we've no reason to suppose any sort of link between a moral belief's being adaptive and its being true. I believe this is why Professor Ruse speaks of "explaining away the foundations of substantive ethics" (p. 67). The point is sharpened when he observes that "we could as easily have evolved a completely different moral system from that which we have" (p. 65). Darwin too considered this possibility. He thought that any social animal graced with a certain degree of rationality would develop a moral sense or conscience. But he did not suppose any necessity to the specific deliverances of conscience.

> If . . . men were reared under precisely the same conditions as hive-bees, there can hardly be a doubt that our unmarried females would, like the worker-bees, think it a sacred duty to kill their brothers, and mothers would strive to kill their fertile daughters, and no one would think of interfering.[3]

Some creaturely characteristics may be nearly inevitable once certain conditions are laid down. Daniel Dennett notes that stereoscopic vision may be a "forced move" given the challenges that attend mobility. But the "conditions" in which we happened to be "reared" were themselves anything but inevitable, having been influenced by such things as asteroid impacts, climate change, mass extinctions and the presence or absence of competing species—not to mention blind dumb luck. We might, then, easily imagine all sorts of counterfactual moralities where conscience bids acts that, from our perspective, are

---

[3]Charles Darwin, *The Descent of Man: And Selection in Relation to Sex* (1871; reprint, New York: Penguin Classics, 2004), p. 122.

outright atrocities. A natural conclusion is that the human morality that has, in fact, emerged is no more "true" than any of those counter-factual moralities. Like the libido, incisors and opposable thumbs, human morality is but another evolved device that has been instrumental toward human survival.

I agree conditionally with Professor Ruse. If we assume the truth of both evolution and Professor Ruse's naturalism, then something close to Professor Ruse's conclusion seems to follow. But I do not share his commitment to naturalism, and, because of this, I think that his skeptical conclusions—and their attending difficulties—are avoidable.

You and I and Professor Ruse operate on a daily basis with deeply engrained moral beliefs that regulate our behaviors and attitudes. Each of us believes, for instance, that killing is wrong. And Professor Ruse goes on to explain, "When I say 'killing is wrong,' I don't just mean that I feel that killing is wrong. I mean that killing truly is absolutely, objectively wrong" (p. 68). I agree. But how can a professed moral nihilist say with a straight face that, despite the fact that he believes that nothing is objectively right or wrong, he also believes that some things are objectively right or wrong? It appears to be a case of the left lobe not knowing what the right lobe is doing.

His answer is to distinguish between *phenomenological* beliefs, on the one hand, and *philosophical* beliefs, on the other. Professor Ruse asserts that his position is "precisely like that of David Hume," who played backgammon and made merry with friends whose very existence was the subject of philosophical doubt. As Hume observed, the propensity to assent to the beliefs of common life always reasserts itself against the skeptical conclusions reached in the philosopher's study.

I do not think that Professor Ruse's position is, in fact, precisely like Hume's. And it seems to me that his overall view is of dubious coherence. For one thing, though Professor Ruse appears to use the terms *ethical skepticism* and *moral nihilism* interchangeably, there is good reason to distinguish them. I believe the former applies to Hume, but the latter does not, and the result of seeing this is significant.

Consider what Judith Thomson calls the "Thesis of Moral Objec-

tivity" (TMO).[4] It is possible to find out about some moral sentences
that they are true. Embedded within TMO are both a metaphysical
thesis ("Some moral sentences are true") and an epistemological thesis
("We can find out"). There are two ways of denying TMO. One may
challenge the metaphysical claim and argue either that they are never
true (noncognitivism, error theory) or that their truth is not mind independent (varieties of constructivism). Or one might challenge the
epistemological claim and deny that any ethical statement is ever justified, so that there is no moral knowledge (even if there are unknow-
able moral truths).

Strictly speaking, the latter is the position of the ethical skeptic, and
such skepticism is closer to Humean skepticism. I think it would be a
mistake to read Hume as offering positive views in metaphysics that
have him asserting, say, the nonexistence of causal connections or a
bundle theory of personal identity (akin to the Buddhist doctrine of
anatman). Rather, in such discussions he argues that (1) the beliefs of
common life are without philosophical justification, and (2) our persis-
tence in holding such unjustified beliefs is explained by appeal to certain human propensities. *Perhaps* there is more to personal identity than
bundles of perceptions that arise in certain patterns with some regular-
ity, but this is all that we are entitled to believe given the available evidence.[5] I think there is a seamless move from Hume's discussion of
these topics to that of moral beliefs. If this is correct, Hume is no more
urging a positive theory of metaethics than he is of metaphysics.

Professor Ruse, on the other hand, *does* have a metaethical theory on
offer, and it is one that denies that there are any mind independent
moral facts. But then we find him testifying to belief in an "absolute"
and "objective" morality. It may be sensible to say, as I take Hume to
say, "I lack philosophical justification for *P*, but *P seems* to be true and
so I believe *P*." And exit polls after church services reveal such to be a
majority view among parishioners. But what can it mean to say, "I *know*

---

[4]Gilbert Harman and Judith Jarvis Thomson, *Moral Relativism and Moral Objectivity* (Oxford:
   Blackwell, 1996), p. 68.
[5]I should add that Hume's view implies that we do not even have an *idea* of such things, as there
   is no impression from which the idea could arise. The same will be true for Hume of the putative idea of objective moral properties.

that *P* is false, but *P seems* to be true and so I *believe P*." As Huck Finn might say, "This is too many for me." Nor do I see how the distinction between phenomenological and philosophical beliefs is of any help. Were you to enter my office to find me hanging from a chandelier, you would think it odd for me to explain that I *believe*, phenomenologically, that there is a man-eating crocodile that I *know*, philosophically, is not there. Professor Ruse's moral faith appears to follow Pudd'nhead Wilson's maxim: "Faith is believing what you know ain't so."

Beyond this, the view seems to suffer at the hands of what John Hare has called the "Publicity Standard": "A normative theory should be able to make public what it claims as the source or origin of the normative demand, without thereby undercutting the demand."[6] Professor Ruse tells us, "If we knew that morality was subjective and that we could ignore it, then very quickly morality would break down and people would start cheating and there would be general mayhem" (p. 68). But he apparently *does* know—or thinks that he knows—this, and he has published this opinion rather widely. He trusts that human psychology is strong enough to ensure that people will *not* ignore the voice of conscience, even if they have come to believe that morality is groundless. I do not share his confidence. As C. S. Lewis once quipped, "Now that I know that my impulse to serve posterity is just the same kind of thing as my fondness for cheese—now that I know that its transcendental pretensions have been exposed for a sham—do you think I shall pay much attention to it?"[7] Hare cites a study concluding that a belief in the theory of psychological egoism (as urged in introductory economics courses) has a tendency to undercut altruistic behavior. He adds, "I speculate that the same would be true after a semester of Professor Ruse's philosophy course."[8]

Professor Ruse claims that his skeptical conclusions follow from the denial that evolution is "progressive" in any way. I agree. Unguided evolution has no prevision of the ends that it achieves, including hu-

---

[6]John Hare, "Is There an Evolutionary Foundation for Human Morality?" Calvin College, www.calvin.edu/academic/philosophy/virtual_library/articles/hare_john/is_there_an_evolutionary_foundation_for_human_morality.pdf, p. 100.

[7]C. S. Lewis, *Miracles* (New York: Harper Collins, 2001), p. 59.

[8]Hare, "Is There an Evolutionary Foundation?" p. 102.

manity. We are neither the pinnacle of the process, nor are our values more than "the inevitable and hygienic bias of one race of animals," as George Santayana once put it.[9] Professor Ruse values people over penguins and pigs, but he does not suppose them to be of greater moral worth. Rather, such valuing comes as standard equipment for most members of his species. John Stuart Mill said that it is better to be a human being dissatisfied than a pig satisfied. But the pig is likely of a different opinion, and any doctrine worthy of swine may be, to him, *sacra doctrina*.

In order to speak of evolutionary progress in any meaningful sense one would require a teleology that has no place within Ruse's version of naturalism. The theist, on the other hand, offers a different reckoning of things. Theism—or something like theism—provides the metaphysical underpinnings that would support a robust version of moral realism. In his critique of Bertrand Russell's early attempt at wedding moral realism with his naturalism, Santayana argued that without the supposition that nature is directed by a cause with a moral interest in the world, nature would exist "for no reason" and would be "deaf to this moral emphasis in the eternal" that Russell supposed himself to discern. He observes,

> The whole Platonic and Christian scheme, in making the good independent of private will and opinion, by no means makes it independent of the direction of nature in general and of human nature in particular. For all things have been created with an innate predisposition towards the creative good and are capable of finding happiness in nothing else. Obligation, in this system, remains internal and vital. Plato attributes a single vital direction and a single narrow source to the cosmos. This is what determines and narrows the source of the true good; for the true good is that relevant to nature. Plato would not have been a dogmatic moralist had he not been a theist.[10]

Like Professor Ruse, I find certain of my moral beliefs to be irresist-

---

[9]George Santayana, *Winds of Doctrine and Platonism and the Spiritual Life* (New York: Harper, 1957), p. 274.
[10]Ibid., p. 143n.

ible. I too believe that killing is "absolutely, objectively wrong." Unlike Professor Ruse, I need not suppose a great divorce between my humanity and my philosophy when it comes to such beliefs. As a theist I believe that human persons have been fashioned in the image of God, and their moral faculties have been designed for the purpose of discerning moral truth. This is one difference that theism makes.

3

Moral Essentialism

Keith E. Yandell

Misty, an accomplished torturer, plies her trade on Mary, whose screams delight her assailant. This is no effort to extract where a bomb has been hidden or when an attack is planned. It is simply for Misty's sadistic pleasure, which Misty intentionally and freely pursues. I venture the suggestion that Misty acts wrongly. If this is so, then it is true that:

(A) If Misty acts wrongly, then in any circumstance in which Mike and Bob (who are like Misty and Mary in all morally relevant respects) are together in an environment that is like Misty's and Mary's in all morally relevant features, and Mike tortures Bob simply for pleasure, then Mike acts wrongly.

(B) If Misty and Mike perform actions that differ in no morally relevant way in circumstances that differ in no morally relevant way, and themselves differ in no morally relevant way, then if they are treated differently with regard to their acts of torture, this is unjust.

Note that differences in personality, endurance, fragility and the like may well be morally relevant, say, to the sort of punishment that Misty and Mike get. Rather than spend all my space presenting counter-examples and replying to them, I will take it that the basic ideas in (A) and (B) are both sound and sufficiently clear.

(A) is a principle of logical consistency, (B) is a principle of justice. If (A) is true, then it is necessarily true—torture simply for pleasure is wrong anywhere, anytime. If (B) is true, it is true because justice requires treating cases in which moral issues arise, and between which there is no morally relevant difference, in the same manner. Then (B) is a necessary truth about justice. Neither (A) nor (B) is merely a statement about the meaning of words or the products of our decisions. If they are true, they are true independent of us and our actions, though of course both (A) and (B) could be put differently in English. I take it, then, that morals are objective in nature.

INTRODUCTION

Views on God and morality range from saying that without God, there is no morality—perhaps because there is no Giver of moral law, perhaps because to be good is simply what God wills—to asserting that, with God, there is no morality—perhaps because if God exists we are not free and hence not morally responsible for anything, perhaps because the concept of God is embroidered with such notions as jealousy and weakness to bribes with the result that religion corrupts morality. Theistic religion is presupposed by morality, or theistic religion destroys morality. The contrast could scarcely be sharper. Then, of course, there are views that fall between the extremes.

The views of ethics also range widely from the view that what we call ethics is created by us to the view that what defines ethics is a set of necessarily true moral principles that are accessible via rational reflection. Both cultural and ethical relativism are brought in to shore up the range of views that fall toward the "we made it up" end of the spectrum. There is not space here to consider either sort of relativism in any detail, but something should be said about them.

CULTURAL AND ETHICAL RELATIVISM

Any sort of relativism says that something is relative to something else. Cultural relativism (CR) says:

> Truth is relative to culture.

One restricted version of CR says:

> Mathematical calculations and geometrical theorems hold good universally in all cultures and countries, but such is not the case with

philosophical doctrines and theories (including ethical theories). In other words, the former is not culture-bound, while the latter is.

On this view, ethical principles cannot be true, period; at best, they can only be something like true-in-a-culture-at-a-given-period-of-time. Problems abound. First, CR is a crosscultural philosophical claim. So on its own grounds, it cannot be true. Second, if you try to argue for (CR) the argument will begin with descriptive relativism:

(DR) Different cultures include incompatible claims.

This further premise is both needed and false:

If DC then CR.

What will come next? Claims from math and science will not do. The premise *propositions that are not crossculturally accepted are not true* is itself not crossculturally accepted. The added premises will have to be universal philosophical claims in order to justify CR and will be disqualified by CR itself from being crossculturally true. Third, consider: physicalism (everything, including persons, is purely material) and dualism (both material and immaterial things exist, persons being at least partly the latter) are logically incompatible philosophical claims. But in whatever sense of truth remains in CR, both can be true, one in one culture and the other in another. Persons in a physicalist culture will be of a different kind than persons in a dualist culture. A person who is unhappy about being purely material can change that by changing cultures. Disease in a culture could be destroyed by altering its relevant beliefs. But these things are neither accepted in our culture nor true, period. In order to play its intended role in our thought and life, CR must be true, period. Those who hold CR do not just mean that CR is true in their culture. They mean that, like DR, CR is true, period. There seem to be two relevant possibilities. "True in a culture" means "accepted as true in a culture"—which requires that "true" bear the sense that they reject. Or "true-in-a-culture" means that anything having that feature is true, period. But this is self-defeating, as well as false.

ETHICAL RELATIVISM

Ethical relativism, in effect, is the result of applying cultural relativism to ethics. Here is one example:

> The recognition of cultural relativism carries with it its own values.
> . . . We shall arrive then at a more realistic social faith, accepting as
> grounds of hope and as new bases for tolerance the coexisting and
> equally valid patterns of life which mankind has created for itself
> from the raw materials of human existence.[1]

First, if ethical relativism brings its own values, it relativizes them in the process. On relativism's own terms, its values are no more "valid" than those of a child molester. Second, it cannot consistently object to any values different from those it embraces. The strongest rebuttal it can consistently make is to the effect that its culture does not happen to accept the value that they are rejecting. Why should those who hold that value care? Third, on this view there is nothing intrinsically wrong. Dining on, rather than with, a relativist is, in itself, morally neutral. Fourth, there is the expectation that the result of embracing relativism will be greater tolerance. This naive myth is exploded by historical example.

> In Italy, relativism is simply a fact. . . . Everything I have said and done
> in these last years is relativism by intuition. . . . From the fact that all
> ideologies are mere fictions, the moral relativist infers that everybody
> has the right [sic] to create for himself his own ideology and to attempt
> to enforce it with all the energy of which he is capable.[2]

Descriptive cultural relativism does not entail normative cultural relativism, and no more favors "nice" mores than it does "vicious" mores. All of this has been said against relativism and thus in favor of the objectivity of morals.

ETHICS AND METAPHYSICS

Metaphysics (theory of reality) is related to ethics in at least two ways. One concerns the sort of freedom we must have if we are morally re-

---

[1]Ruth Benedict, *Patterns of Culture* (Boston: Houghton Mifflin, 1934), p. 278.
[2]Benito Mussolini, *Diuturna* (Milan: Alpes, 1924), pp. 374-77.

sponsible. Another concerns what, if anything, exists that has value, and why it has value. This concern is, or is close to, asking the question, What makes moral propositions, particularly moral principles, true? Divine command theorists respond, in various ways, that the answer is to be found in what God wills.

The Euthyphro dilemma. One argument for the autonomy of ethics from religion starts from the old dilemma taken from the Platonic dialogue *Euthyphro*. Succinctly, it goes: either the good is good because the gods choose it or the gods choose it because it is good. We can easily revise this so that it applies to monotheism: either God arbitrarily decides what is good or bad, right or wrong, or what is good or bad, right or wrong, is determined by something independent of God's choice. In the former case, nothing is intrinsically good or bad, right or wrong. In the latter, God's sovereignty is compromised. Either alternative is incompatible with traditional monotheism. So ethics is autonomous from religion. This has been taught in countless introductory courses in philosophy and ethics.

The argument is a dilemma: there are just two possibilities. Neither is compatible with ethics being based on monotheism. So ethics cannot be, and so is not, based on monotheism. A dilemma argument is successful only if the alternatives presented exhaust all possibilities. Offering only two possibilities, this dilemma does not.

(1) The good is determined by arbitrary divine choice.

This is so because otherwise God's choice is a function of something that exists independent of God. Or,

(2) God's choice that something is good is based on something over which God has no control.

If so, then God is not sovereign.

Thought of in these terms, the dilemma is supposed to prove that theists have three choices. One is to hold that God is an arbitrary ruler. The second is to hold that God is subject to a law not of God's own making. The third is to hold that ethics is autonomous, free from any religious basis. The third alternative seems the least unattractive to theists. So theists ought to grant that ethics is not dependent on religion.

Two further alternatives. As we noted, in order to have this sort of impact, the Euthyphro dilemma must cover all the bases. This one does not do so. Here are two more alternatives:

(3) What is good is determined by God's choice, and God's choice is based on God's nature, which is perfectly good.

(4) What is good is not determined by God's choice, but by God's nature, which is perfectly good.

According to (3), God's choice is the basis of morality, but it is not arbitrary. According to (4) God's choice is not the ground of morality, but God's nature is. While (3) and (4) are not identical—on (4), God need not make a choice—they are obviously closely related. We will look at their connection shortly.

A closer look at alternative two. Alternative (2) deserves a closer look. It may be helpful to consider a similar issue by way of comparison. Consider a standard example of a logical truth in the philosophical tradition:

The principle of noncontradiction: (a) no proposition can be both true and false; (b) nothing can have logically incompatible properties.

According to Aristotle, this is a law of thought and of things. Our statement of the principle of noncontradiction (PNC) needs a bit of explanation. The (a) statement has to do with propositions. A proposition is anything that possesses truth value in the primary sense. The truth value of a proposition is simply its being true or false. There are no degrees of truth and falsehood, and what is sometimes put in terms of such degrees is really a degree of approximation to truth or to falsehood. On one account, propositions exist independent of our ever thinking of them, asserting or denying them, or being related to them in any way at all. That there were dinosaurs, that two plus seven are nine, that if there are persons it is wrong to torture them for pleasure were true before we were around to think about them. That there sometime would be dinosaurs has always been true, though it might have been false. That two plus seven are nine has always been true, and it cannot have been false.

On this view, then, there are propositions and they are mind independent. Among these propositions, some—we have two examples—are necessarily true, true in all possible worlds, true no matter what way the world goes. One philosophical way of talking about such propositions is that they are abstract objects—things that exist necessarily, are everlasting (or eternal), are not located in space and are mind-independent. If we ask what ontological or metaphysical status the PNC has, the answer will be that it is a necessarily true proposition.

If we follow this general line of reasoning—one that I think is correct, though it requires more discussion than space permits—we can add either of two views that render it more specific:

A. Propositions are necessarily existing abstract objects that can neither be created nor destroyed.

B. What some refer to as abstract objects are in fact the propositional contents of thoughts that a necessarily existing Mind necessarily has.

The thought that chocolate is grand has, as its propositional content, that chocolate is grand. The principle of noncontradiction is the propositional content of the thought that the principle of noncontradiction is true. On view B, propositions are propositional contents of divine ideas. This view was held, for example, by Augustine, who—in a history of philosophy slogan that is actually correct—"placed Plato's abstract objects in the mind of God."

Suppose A is the correct view. I take it that if the existence of some item X is caused to exist, it is possible that it not have existed as well as possible that it existed, and whatever causes X explains why it is that the possibility of its existence is the one that holds. If this is correct, then abstract objects—in particular, propositions—cannot be caused to exist. Since for God to be omnipotent is not for God to be able to make contradictions true, even God cannot create propositions.

Finally, note that on view A, the PNC is a necessary truth. It exists independent of God, since it exists independent of anything whatever if it exists at all. The relevant question here is whether this limits divine sovereignty. I suggest that it does not. Any proper doctrine of divine sovereignty is going to be true, and thus possibly true—that is, not a necessary falsehood. But it is a necessary falsehood that a contradiction be true. So if it is a necessary falsehood that a proposition be created, then a possibly true account of divine sovereignty will not entail that propositions can be created by God. Thus a true account of divine sovereignty will not assert otherwise.

Now we can return to our main topic. Suppose—as I take to be true—that the fundamental principles of ethics are necessarily true. For example, it is a necessary truth that if there are persons, then they ought to be respected, at least unless they have so acted as to forfeit that right. (Whether that is possible we need not inquire.) If it is a necessarily true proposition, then God cannot create (or destroy) it. Suppose the A view is true. Thus the truth of fundamental moral principles will not depend on God. But is this something that refutes the theist?

This obviously depends on what sort of theism one has in mind. The relevant point here is whether one accepts:

Theism 1: If X exists, and X is not God, then God created X. (It does not follow that God created everything that God could create.)

Theism 2: If X exists, and X is not God, then God has created every X unless it is not possible that X be created.

The difference between Theism 1 and Theism 2 is that, if one thinks that there are necessarily existing things that cannot be created, one should accept Theism 2.

It is worth taking a moment to fine-tune the notion of divine omnipotence. Here is one rendition:

God is omnipotent entails that if proposition P is not a necessary falsehood, *God makes P true* is not a necessary falsehood, *God makes P true* is not incompatible with God having some property that God has essentially, and God is not precluded from making P true because of God being who God is, then God can make P true.

So that seven plus two are forty, that there is an uncreated universe, that God breaks God's promises, and that God writes your autobiography as autobiography are not things that even an omnipotent God can realize. The definition of divine omnipotence must be logically consistent. Note that, given the characterization just stated, and given the assumption that things that have logically necessary existence cannot be created, Theism 2 is compatible with God being omnipotent. While the characterization of omnipotence offered here may not be the last word on the topic, I think it is the case that this much should be included. My conclusion here, in any case, is that a theist can perfectly well live with Theism 2 and thus with alternative 2 of the dilemma.

The result thus far is that the Euthyphro dilemma is a failure because it is an incomplete list of the relevant alternatives, and one of the actually proposed alternatives is compatible with a robust theism.

Divine command theories fine-tuned. The conceptual map of divine command theories needs a bit more fine-tuning. There are divine command theories of the good and divine command theories of the right that include at least the following:

(5) Choice voluntarism: What is good is decided by an arbitrary divine choice—were the choice not arbitrary, then there would be something that determined or partly determined what is good other than divine choice, and this is impossible.

(6) Choice by nature: What is good is decided by a nonarbitrary divine choice—the criterion of what is good is decided by God's nature, by properties that God has essentially.

An important difference between (5) and (6) is that on (5), what is good and what is evil could have been (and presumably can be) different, or even reversed, whereas on (6) this is not so. There is no reason, on (5), to suppose that a type of action may not be good one day and evil the next, or good in leap years but not in other years, and so on. Whether being inconsistent in this matter is good, bad or neutral is arbitrarily decided.

It is worth noting that for voluntarism, not even revelation can give us anything we can be confident is an ethical truth. The Bible is opposed to blasphemy. But if voluntarism is true, for all we know God populates heaven only with blasphemers because God loves only them. After all, God may have arbitrarily decided that what we think is particularly bad—lying about important matters, for example—is particularly good. Thinking consistently, acting consistently with what one promises and acting justly may have no value, or have negative value. It all depends on God's arbitrary choice. It seems that voluntarists assume that once God has said that something is good or bad, then it stays good or bad. This is an arbitrary assumption on the part of voluntarists.

(7) Choice conceptualism: What is good is determined by a set of necessary truths that are made true by thoughts that a necessarily existing God cannot fail to have; the propositional content of these thoughts are necessary truths that define what is good—that express the nature of the good.

(8) Choice determined by abstracta: What is good is determined by abstract objects—say, propositions—that define what is good, and in accord with which God chooses what God shall regard as good.

This is *essentialist ethics*. If it is true, it is necessarily true.

There are four corresponding divine command theories of the right or the obligatory. They are views in which *good* is replaced by *obligatory* or by *what ought to be, or be done*. They go as follows:

(5*) Choice voluntarism: What is obligatory, or what ought to be or be done, is decided by an arbitrary divine choice—were the choice not arbitrary, then there would be something that determined or partly determined what is obligatory, or what ought to be or be done, other than divine choice, and this is impossible.

(6*) Choice by nature: What is obligatory, or what ought to be or be done, is decided by a nonarbitrary divine choice—the criterion of what is obligatory, or what ought to be or be done, is decided by God's nature, by properties that God has essentially. God's choice in this regard is determined by God's nature.

An important difference between (5*) and (6*) is that on (5*) what is obligatory, or what ought to be or be done, and what ought not to be or be done, could have been (and presumably can be) different, or even reversed, whereas on (6*) this is not so.

(7*) Choice conceptualism: What is obligatory, or what ought to be or be done, is determined by a set of necessary truths that are made true by thoughts that a necessarily existing God cannot fail to have; the propositional content of these thoughts are necessary truths that define what is obligatory, or what ought to be or be done—that express the nature of the obligatory, or what ought to be or be done.

(8*) Choice determined by abstracta: What is obligatory, or what ought to be or be done, is determined by abstract objects—say, propositions—that define what is obligatory, or what ought to be or be done, and in accord with which God chooses what God shall regard as obligatory, or what ought to be or be done.

This again is moral essentialism, here about "ought" and "right." If it is true, it is necessarily true.

Moral essentialism holds that a true moral principle is necessarily true. It claims that necessary truths are mind-independently necessary. Thus they are not true in virtue of linguistic convention, "deep grammar," the way our mind or brain works, or sociological agreement. Anything true in virtue of any of these would not be a necessary truth, as any of these might not have existed. The same goes for the principles of logic. Empiricists typically hold that necessary truths are true in virtue of some such thing as those just mentioned. They thus deny that necessary truths are necessarily true. One argument for an empiricist view of this sort is the alleged impossibility of our otherwise knowing necessary truths. Neither God nor abstract objects are accessible to sensory or introspective experience. But then neither is the truth of *We cannot know anything whose truth is not based on objects of sensory or introspective experience accessible in this manner.* Giving a positive account of our knowledge of necessary truths is not possible here; it is a substantial topic by itself. Suffice it to say that the position that necessary truths are mind-independently so has a long history of exposition and defense by first-rate philosophers.

Voluntarism. The voluntarist views are problematic. They are versions of a "might makes right" doctrine—what is good or right is whatever someone with sufficient power says is good or right. But *X is good or right* neither entails nor is entailed by *X is good or right in the view of a person of great power.* It follows from voluntarism that nothing is intrinsically good or right, or bad or wrong; the choice by the power that is said to determine the good and the right is arbitrary in the sense that it could equally well not have been made or not been made as it was. Hitler might have been a moral saint without any other change in him whatever—having held the same beliefs, made the same choices, done the same things, all from the same motives, and be at least close to moral perfection. Mother Theresa might have been the model of wicked depravity. Nor is there the comfort that at least God did not decide in a manner that yielded that result. There is no nonarbitrary reason why God should not have decided that beginning tomorrow Hitler will be saintly and Theresa depraved. There is no duty to be steadfast in a decision once it is made. Even an arbitrary decision not to change one's decision, made by God yesterday, can be overturned today by an equally arbitrary choice to rescind that decision. God has no inherent moral character, and none is gained by proper use of free choice, since God can elect to be what now would be immoral but will not according to the new set of rules. *God is good* means something like *God meets God's arbitrary standard of goodness*. That standard may be one that defines goodness as torturing for pleasure on even numbered days and being horrified by the thought of doing so on odd numbered days, or refraining from murder until one is eighteen and then becoming a serial killer. This has seemed to many theists an inadequate view of God and of morality. Were it true, so-called ethics would be merely a risky prudence of not displeasing God in a context where what was pleasing might change at any moment, and where pleasing God might not be helpful to you in any case, since God might treat those who pleased God worse than anyone else. This leaves us with three views regarding the good and three regarding the right.

PRINCIPLED DIVINE COMMANDS

On the principled divine commands view, God's commands determine what is good or right, but they are not arbitrary. They are made in accord with God's nature. One way of understanding this involves the notion of an essence. Each thing that exists has an essence; it is good that it exists and also good that it becomes a fully mature member of the species into which its essence puts it. There are distinctive capacities grounded in the essential properties of a thing, and it is good that it develops those capacities in a way that comports with its nature and leads it to being a model member of its species. Created persons more resemble God than any other created beings, and it is especially good that they become flourishing persons. God—if we may speak of a necessarily one-membered kind—is a perfect exemplar of divinity and the supreme good. Created persons, by proper use of reason, choice and action (and by grace) can come to resemble God as much as is possible for them. God's commandments specify central features of a life that leads to this goal. Since the purpose of the commandments is to produce flourishing persons, and this flourishing is resembling God as much as is possible, the divine nature shapes the content of the commandments. Since flourishing involves imitating God, so far as this is possible, it requires deep concern for the flourishing of other persons and involvement in helping others toward that end. This gives a rough brief sketch of how commands that define basic moral principles can be related to the nature of God, in terms of the good, the right or both.

Divine nature as exemplar. The divine nature as exemplar view might roughly be described as the previous view, minus commands. What is good is determined and measured by God's nature. Being as like God as it is possible for persons to become is the good for persons, and if we have obligations, they concern our becoming, and helping others become, persons of this sort. There are views on which the doctrine of the good is the core of ethics, and no reference to "right" or "obligation" is required, save where speaking of the "right" thing to do means the thing it is "good" to do. (Perhaps it should be noted that, largely under the influence of one or more schools of philosophy, various Jewish and Christian thinkers have declared knowledge of the essence of God to be impossible, at least in this lifetime. This is typically closely connected with—even a consequence of—the notion of divine simplicity, which roughly is the view that for any two predicates—say "omnipotent" and "loving"—that are true of God, they refer to the same thing in God. For any two properties P and Q that are misleading but not utterly inappropriate to ascribe to God, P and Q are the same property and both are identical to God, who is identical to God's essence. This is not the place to discuss the controversial notion of divine simplicity.)

The abstracta view. I have suggested that the abstracta view is not somehow disastrous for or inconsistent with a robust monotheism. For God to be fully sovereign is for God to have control over all created things. In addition, propositions—like all abstract objects—lack consciousness and causal power. They are not potential rebels. On this account, God need not have logically necessary existence, though God will still have the property of not depending for existence on any cause. (If God is held to have logically necessary existence, then it is puzzling why one of the previous nonvoluntarist views is not being held.) The idea is that the first moral principle or principles are rationally accessible to us.

There are certain ways in which, for most theisms, God and morality are related. One is that only if God creates moral agents has ethics any application to creatures. Suppose that the basic principles of ethics are necessary truths. Still, they are all conditional—as are "if there are persons, then they ought to be respected" and "if there are sentient creatures, then they ought not to be tortured for pleasure." Even if these are necessary truths, they apply to a world only if there are persons or sentient creatures in it. Otherwise, they are axioms of an irrelevant system. The theist holds that if there are moral agents, then God created them, and so ethics has purchase on the world only if God not only creates but creates certain sorts of beings.

Theists also hold that God is good, typically at least including moral goodness. A theist may hold that God is morally good by nature or by choice. It is important here to distinguish between metaphysical worth and moral worth. It is widely held that persons have metaphysical worth just in virtue of being persons. Both Aristotle and Kant, different though their views are in some ways, hold this. The Platonic tradition takes it that anything has metaphysical worth simply in virtue of existing, and that there is a natural order in which higher things have more value than lower things. Metaphysical worth is not earned; it comes along with just existing, even for God. It is a function of one's nature, and nothing determines its own basic nature—the metaphysical kind to which it belongs. Not carrots, comets, collies or even God.

There is also moral worth, which for Aristotle and Kant is earned over time through voluntary actions. This can and does vary between members of the same kind and requires rationality in some strong sense of that complex term. A theist will hold that God is metaphysically perfect by nature. He or she may hold that God is morally perfect by nature or that God is morally perfect by choice. The latter view has been less popular, but popularity is not a test for truth. The metaphysical/moral distinction is often not raised in discussion of these matters, and it is not obvious that metaphysical perfection entails moral perfection. It is also controversial whether moral perfection by nature is possible, since it is often held to be available only to moral agents, who must be possessed of libertarian freedom—and no one is libertarianly free with regard to what is included among his or her essential properties. If God is eternal (timeless) then it is harder, if not impossible, to see that God's moral goodness be gained from libertarian freedom. Nonetheless, a good many contemporary Christian philosophers have held that God is everlasting rather than timeless.[3] Further, it is typically held that God could, in some strong sense of *could*, have refrained from creating at all, without this making God less metaphysically or morally magnificent than otherwise. It is sometimes argued that a perfectly rational being would never choose or act wrongly, and God is perfectly rational, and the metaphysical perfection of perfect rationality entails moral perfection. But this simply shifts the focus of the difference. God is granted to be rationally perfect in the sense of committing no fallacies or having any false beliefs. But a libertarianly free being with respect to ethics could elect to go against reason and choose or act wrongly without making an intellectual mistake in so doing. The idea that such a being would always act as the application of moral principles required in the way that a rational creature cannot withhold belief from a clearly perceived necessary truth simply recites the rejection of a metaphysically perfect being having libertarian freedom regarding

---

[3]See Gregory E. Ganssle, ed., *God and Time: Four Views* (Downers Grove, Ill.: IVP Academic, 2001).

moral matters. Of course if you assume that, you can then derive it from itself without difficulty (and without merit).

One obligation can be greater than another. If I have promised to lend you a novel so you can read it for a pleasant evening, and promised Tom that I will drive him to a crucial doctor's appointment, and I have not noticed that these tasks conflict, then my duty is to take Tom to the doctor. If I have also promised Tom's family that I will do so, my already weighty obligation becomes even stronger. Similarly, if I ought not to steal anyway, and God also commands me not to steal, my obligation not to steal becomes greater, since God has given me life and the ability both to steal and to refrain from stealing, which requires various good gifts in terms of abilities and powers.

A more complex view is possible. Consider these brief statements of views, shorter versions of ones already noted:

C. What is good is determined by necessarily true propositions.

C*. Doing what is good is commanded by God.

D. What ought to be or be done is determined by necessarily true propositions.

D*. What ought to be or be done is commanded by God.

Suppose both C and D are true. Then ask: Does the fact that it is good that X be done entail that, if I can (and there are no at least equally good alternatives), then I ought to do X? There is a school of ethics that holds that not only is a doctrine of the good fundamental to ethics, but that there is no need for obligation. On this view, anyway, that it is good—even better than any alternative—that you do X, does not entail that you ought to do X. But suppose that obligations are always owed to someone, and most of all to God, if there are any such things as obligations. Add that you know that God has commanded that X be done by such as you in circumstances of the sort in which you find yourself. Then you will be obligated to do X in a way you are not so obligated if it is merely good that X be done.

Suppose D is true. Then what ought to be or be done is not defined in terms of what God wills that you do. But that God wills that you do

X may still bring about an obligation on your part to do *X*. This may be because you ought to do *X* anyway, and God's commanding you to do so makes the obligation stronger.

Alternatively, suppose that doing *X* in and of itself is neither good nor bad, neither what ought to be or be done, nor what ought not—it is morally neutral. Still, God's commanding that you do *X* may create an obligation that you do *X*, since God is your heavenly Father. So there are several relations between God and morality even if the divine command theories are not true.

METAPHYSICS AGAIN

If ethical principles are made true by divine command or nature, and these principles are necessarily true, God must exist necessarily and necessarily command as God does. The idea that God exists necessarily has been multiply explored in contemporary philosophy. The varieties of modality are necessity, possibility and contingency. These are properties of propositions. A proposition is a necessary truth only if it is not possible that it be false. Necessary falsehoods cannot be true. Logically contingent propositions can be either true or false. Possible propositions are propositions that can be true. An issue regarding modality is relevant here. In medieval philosophy, it was typically held that God's existence is necessary—not necessary *for* something but intrinsically necessary. What exactly this means is less clear.

At least part of what it means is that God is causally independent and indeed cannot have a cause. It is also taken to mean that it is self-contradictory to say that God does not exist. This latter notion requires some analysis. One sort of necessity is formal logical necessity. This is a property of propositions that have certain logical structures. For example, consider the sentence frame *If X is Q and Q*, then X is Q*, an ordinary example being *If Bill is broad and tall, then Bill is broad*. This sentence does not assert that Bill does exist, only that if he does and is broad and tall, then he is broad. Its denial has the structure *X can be Q and Q* and not be Q*, which is impossible. There is another sort of necessity that we will call informal logical necessity. It is a property that propositions have in virtue of their meaning; for example, *Orange re-*

sembles red more than it resembles green and *Nothing can simultaneously be red all over and green all over.* (There are more philosophical examples, such as *If X is identical to Y then X is necessarily identical to Y.*)

"God does exist" is not a logically necessary truth; it lacks a formally contradictory denial. "God, who exists, does not exist" is formally contradictory, but so is "Santa Claus, who exists, does not exist," and this is no proof of the existence of Santa. If we consider informal logical necessity we may get further. Consider this line of reasoning:

Definition 1: A necessary truth is a proposition that is true in every way a world might be.

Definition 2: A maximal proposition is a proposition P such that, for any proposition Q, either P entails Q or P entails *not-Q*.

Definition 3: A maximal proposition describes a total way a world might be.

Definition 4: God has maximal excellence if God is omnipotent, omniscient and morally perfect in at least one way a world might be.

Definition 5: God has maximal greatness if God has maximal excellence in every way a world might be.

Now the argument:

(9) Either *God is omnipotent, omniscient and morally perfect in every way a world might be* is possibly true or *God is omnipotent, omniscient and morally perfect in every way a world might be* is not possibly true.

(10) If *God is omnipotent, omniscient and morally perfect in every way a world might be* is not possibly true, then the concept of God (as in definition 5) is contradictory.

(11) The concept of God (as in definition 5) is not contradictory.

(12) It is possibly true that *God is omnipotent, omniscient and morally perfect in every way a world might be.*

(13) If it is possibly true that *God is omnipotent, omniscient and morally perfect in every way a world might be*, then *God is omnipotent, omniscient and morally perfect in every way a world might be* is true.

(14) Therefore, *God is omnipotent, omniscient and morally perfect in every way a world might be* is true.

Regarding the premises: (9) is a necessary truth—for any proposition *P*, either *P* is a necessary truth or it is not; (10) is also a necessary truth—for any proposition *P*, if *P* is not possibly true, then *P* is necessarily false; the reason for accepting this premise is that, upon reflection, there seems no contradiction in the definition; regarding (12), if there is no contradiction in *God is omnipotent, omniscient and morally perfect in every way a world might be* being true, then it is possibly true; regarding (13), *God is omnipotent, omniscient and morally perfect in every way a world might be* is a claim about every way a world might be, and any such claim is either a necessary truth or a necessary falsehood; the conclusion (14) follows from (12) and (13). The argument looks impeccable. In fact, it isn't. Consider:

> Definition 6: God has maximal excellence if God is omnipotent, omniscient and morally perfect in some ways that a world might be but not in others, and exists in this world.

Upon reflection, this definition too seems not contradictory. But if one defines *God* along the lines of definition 6, the argument will not succeed. Premise (10) will then be replaced by something like:

> (10*) God is omnipotent, omniscient and morally perfect in every way a world might be, or God is omnipotent, omniscient and morally perfect in only some ways a world might be.

Premise (10*) will not join (9), (11), (12) and (13) in an argument that yields (14).

What (10*) amounts to is saying that either (i) *God is omnipotent, omniscient and morally perfect in every way a world might be* is a necessary truth (and if not a necessary truth, then a necessary falsehood) or (ii) *God is omnipotent, omniscient and morally perfect in only some ways a world might be* is a logically contingent proposition (whether true or false). The problem with the argument we have stated is that it does not show that (i) is correct and (ii) incorrect.[4]

---

[4]For all this, see also Alvin Plantinga, *God, Freedom and Evil* (Grand Rapids: Eerdmans, 1978).

The (9-14) argument requires definition 5; definition 6 is incompatible with definition 5, though a theist who accepts either can also hold that God cannot possibly be caused. Neither 5 nor 6 seems contradictory, but one must be. The (9-14) argument requires 5, and since it is not clear that it is 5 rather than 6 that is the correct definition, the argument fails. The idea was to prove that *God exists* is a necessary truth in the sense of *God* as given in 5. The fact is that we have no such proof. Hence, that God is an informally necessary being—"God exists" is informally necessarily true—is not proved. But if true ethical principles are necessarily true, then they cannot be true simply in virtue of being the contents of thoughts that God necessarily has if *God exists* is not a necessary truth.

Differently, suppose (N), *No nonabstract object can exist necessarily*, is true. (So far as I know, this is also unproved.) Necessarily, God is not an abstract object. Either (G), *God exists necessarily*, is a necessary truth and (N) is necessarily false, or (N) is necessarily true and (G) is necessarily false; (G) being necessarily false is compatible with God's existence. (It should be remembered that the sort of necessity relevant here is informal logical necessity.) We do not know which of (G) and (N) is true. Thus we do not know that, if ethical principles are necessary truths, then those principles are made true by God's nature or thoughts. They may be true in virtue of being grounded in abstract objects. (If there is only one such principle, the previous sentences can be easily altered to take that into account.) If (N) is true, then—given the previous discussion—at least the nature of the good is determined by abstracta. Then moral essentialism is true. As we have seen, this does not entail that God is unrelated to morality. Analogous remarks apply to the nature of obligation—of what ought to be done and to be.

The moral of this long story is that there is not just one way in which God and ethics can be related. Obviously the question of whether God and ethics are related in any of these ways can be answered affirmatively only if both God and ethics exist. But that was not our topic. My purpose has simply been to outline a view of ethics—moral essentialism—that I take to be attractive and open to both theists and nontheists.

A Naturalist Moral Realism Response

Evan Fales

KEITH YANDELL IS A MORAL REALIST; so am I. In the course of explicating his moral essentialism, Yandell undertakes to defend what he calls the "abstracta view," though he does not declare himself on whether he favors that view. My own view comes close, in important ways, to moral essentialism and especially the abstracta view. So in this reply to Yandell, I will be provoking a few skirmishes, not waging any frontal assault.

Skirmish 1. As noted, I share Yandell's view that moral truths are objective truths. I am, however, less confident of his (very brief) opening argument for that position. It hinges on the correctness of his principle (B), which asserts, roughly, that if two parties engage in actionable moral offenses that don't differ in any morally relevant ways, then their punishments ("treatment") should be the same. I am inclined to agree, but I'm not entirely sure. Peter van Inwagen argues that if a given crime warrants, say, a year's jail sentence, then a sentence of only 364 days is equally justified.[1] But then, if Misty receives a sentence of one year for her crime, and Mike a sentence of only 364 days, has justice not been served? My intuitions are unclear, but perhaps that's because I'm not sure van Inwagen's premise (as adapted for present purposes) is correct. Or perhaps, even if 365 days and 364 days are both fair sentences, it will be unfair if some are punished with the one and some with the other.

Skirmish 2. Second, I have qualms about Yandell's attempt to show that cultural relativism (CR) is somehow self-defeating and cannot in any case be derived from descriptive relativism (DR). It's true that CR is a crosscultural claim. But it doesn't follow that it can't be true. The doughty relativist can allow, without inconsistency, that *it itself* has a truth value that is relative to culture. Moreover, Yandell has not estab-

---

[1]Peter van Inwagen, *The Problem of Evil* (Oxford: Clarendon, 2006), pp. 100-102. Van Inwagen's argument is directed at the comparative efficacies of alternative punishments, not the question of justice. But his argument suggests the adaptation I am considering.

lished that a properly restricted CR can't be established by appeal to
DR. It remains open to the relativist to try to argue for a CR that's restricted to, say, normative ethics, from DR. So long as the putative
demonstration doesn't appeal to alleged crosscultural ethical norms, it
is not self-undermining in the way Yandell envisions. Not being a relativist, I'm happy to leave that project to those who are.

But what about the wide diversity of ethically charged cultural practices? Kung San women of the Kalahari, for example, used to perform
infanticide if a child was born while the previous child was still nursing
(i.e., to about age four). Eskimos reputedly would sometimes abandon
the infirm to die of hypothermia in the Arctic winter. Such practices
are probably not as morally horrific as they seem at first blush. Kung
San women are gatherers; a woman burdened with two babes-in-arms
would have been unable to feed her family. Similarly, Eskimos in circumstances of severe privation would not have been able to support an
infirm elder without serious repercussion for the group as a whole. So
many of these sorts of cases do not cast doubt upon moral realism or
even support cultural (moral) relativism. At most, they reflect the fact
that there are genuinely hard moral dilemmas that people of good will
may settle differently, and that such different resolutions may become
culturally enshrined (which isn't, however, to deny that there are occa-
sionally cultures that go off the rails, morally speaking).

Skirmish 3. Yandell nicely sets out a range of theistic options respecting the relationship between God and morality. Of these, the one
I'll focus my remarks on takes the truths of morality to be conditional
necessary truths, truths of the form "If such-and-such is the case (e.g.,
if there are sentient creatures, persons, etc.), then they are to be treated
in so-and-so ways." Yandell sees such truths, on this account, as *abstracta* whose existence and truth value even an omnipotent God cannot
determine or change.

I largely agree, but with some caveats. First, a minor one: there are
some contingent moral truths. It's a moral truth that Athens should not
have executed Socrates. But this is contingent, as both Athens and
Socrates are not necessary beings. There are more general contingent
truths—for example, that normal human children should be given pa-

rental care until they are twenty years old or so. For it is a contingent truth that this is roughly how long it takes normal human children to reach self-sufficiency. But these are not the sorts of truths that Yandell means to be considering.

Some may be surprised to find an avowed naturalist, such as myself, dallying with abstracta. They should not be: I am also an avowed Platonist; propositions are, happily, denizens of my ontology. The naturalism to which I subscribe is quite minimalist; it is captured by the thesis that there are no disembodied minds. So moral essentialism is consistent with my ontology. (Of course I cannot begin to defend that ontology here.)

Skirmish 4. But I am more interested in the necessary moral truths. Unfortunately, Yandell does not tell us what *kind* of necessity attaches to these truths. It makes a difference. Philosophers distinguish a variety of species of modality: formal logical necessity, analytic truth, "conceptual" necessity, what Yandell calls "informal logical necessity" (his examples include (1) orange is more like red than like green, and (2) nothing can be both red and green all over at the same time), metaphysical necessity and causal necessity—among others. There are debates over which of these exist and which are reducible to others. There are also debates over which sorts of necessity, if any, God has a say in.[2]

I consider it uncontroversial that the necessary moral truths aren't truths of (formal) logic; nor are they analytically true. But perhaps they are metaphysically necessary, or—if that doesn't come to the same thing—perhaps they have the kind of necessity that attaches to "Pink is lighter than red" or "Pink resembles red more closely than it resembles green."

Many theists hold that God is sovereign over the laws of nature: he determines what they shall be. If the laws of nature have modal status—if they reflect what we may call nomic or causal necessities—then certain necessary truths are up to God. If ethical truths have *that* kind of necessity, then God would—on this showing—have control over

---

[2]For a radical view, see Brian Leftow's forthcoming *God and Necessity* (Oxford University Press). Yandell says that (1) and (2) are true in virtue of the meanings of the propositions. I doubt that *propositions* have (or are) meanings; in any event, questions of meaning are vexed. Neither (1) nor (2) seems to be analytically true.

their content in spite of their necessity. Yandell will surely deny that necessary moral truths are nomically necessary. And I would deny that, even if they are, God has control over them: according to me, nomic necessity reduces to metaphysical necessity, and not even God can determine metaphysical necessities.

But we are not out of the woods yet. Cosmological arguments for the existence of God characteristically generate an interesting modal problem. Suppose the argument proceeds from the premise that there are contingent things and events, and appeals to a principle of sufficient reason (PSR) that says, roughly, that every contingent being must have a cause. A regress, variously constructed, takes us to an uncaused first cause which, a fortiori, is a necessary being. Very well. But we may ask, Is this necessary being's causing contingent beings itself a necessary event or a contingent one? If the latter, then it must itself be caused, and the regress is off and running again. But if the former, then our supposedly contingent beings are not contingent after all: they are the necessary effects of the necessary activity of a necessary being. So there will be dependent (i.e., caused) necessary beings—the creatures—and at least one independent, or *a se* necessary being: God. But then, might the propositions that express the moral law be dependent necessary beings—beings it is within God's purview to ordain after all (even if necessarily so)? At least something more needs to be said about the relevant sorts of necessity, if moral essentialism is to receive an adequate defense.[3]

Skirmish 5. As Yandell himself repudiates the ontological argument he presents in the final section of his essay, my heaping on further criticisms is perhaps coals to Newcastle. But I cannot resist a couple of remarks. Consider principle E:

(E) "X has property P in possible world α" entails "X exists in possible world α"

---

[3] A theist can avoid this line of reasoning by suitably restricting her or his PSR. The theist may hold that every contingent event is caused by another event, unless it is a decision freely made by an agent. If the theist then has an agent-causation view of free action, she or he may aver that the free creative acts of God—himself a free agent—are contingently produced by a necessary being (not an event) and produce contingent beings. Yet those acts, though contingent, require no further explanation than that they were agent caused; the regress is halted. Though a libertarian, I am not myself sympathetic with the agent-causation account.

Some modal semantics accept (E); some do not. If one accepts a semantic theory free of assumption (E), then Yandell's (14)—which reads, *"God is omnipotent, omniscient and morally perfect in every way a world might be* is true"—might be true, even though God fails to exist in some possible worlds—including the actual world. For, even if *God is omnipotent, omniscient and morally perfect* is true in every possible world, including the actual world, it will not follow that *God exists.*

But if the concept of God entails that he exists, then the argument is unsound, since premise (11) provides no reason for thinking that God is a possible being, so (10) is false.[4] So the only way to try to rescue the argument is to accept:

(9*) God is omnipotent, etc., in every possible world in which he exists.

and

(9**) Either God exists in some possible world or he does not.

But this does not help: (10) remains false, for God could be an impossible being even though the concept of God is logically consistent.[5]

Skirmish 6. Finally, I want to take issue with a remark Yandell makes that suggests a problematic conception of libertarian freedom. He says,

A libertarianly free being . . . could elect to go against reason and choose . . . wrongly without making an intellectual mistake in so doing. The idea that such a being [as God] would always act as the application of moral principles required . . . simply recites the rejection of a metaphysically perfect being having libertarian freedom regarding moral matters. (p. 111)

---

[4]See William Rowe, *Philosophy of Religion: An Introduction,* 3rd ed. (Belmont, Calif.: Wadsworth, 2001), chap. 3, for a clear exposition of the problem here.

[5]The mistake here is perhaps the mistake of identifying (formal) logical possibility with truth in a possible world. As Saul Kripke showed (I believe), truth in a possible world marks metaphysical possibility. Logical possibility is to be understood as truth on some interpretation. Logical possibility is a merely formal notion; existence in a possible world is an ontological claim. In any case, Yandell's (13) presupposes the S5 axiom $\diamond\Box p \supset \Box p$; (13) and (9) entail that God's existence is either impossible or necessary. So, as Rowe shows, the argument begs the question against the atheist.

I disagree. That is, I disagree that libertarian freedom—"real" freedom, if you will—consists in being able to choose to disobey the rules of reason. Reasoning *itself* is, of course, subject to normative evaluation, and that entails the conceptual coherence of mistake-making. But it does not follow that choosing freely, even if it is conceptually tied to rationality (as I think it is), is to be understood as a capacity for both following and failing to follow proper intellectual hygiene. As I have elsewhere argued, paradigmatically free choosing *just is* the rational execution of a practical syllogism, and the performance of the relevant inferences, though determining the action to be performed, is not a causal process.[6] Ergo, that action is not causally determined. If that is right, then we are the more free, the more rational our practical deliberations. God, who is maximally rational, will therefore be maximally free. He knows all the choices available to him, and he always knows which choice is best—and does it.

Our practical reason, which isn't impeccable, suffers from various defects or species of irrationality. These include, *inter alia*, weakness of the will and mistakes in reasoning (bad inferences, failure to take into consideration known relevant facts, etc.). But does anyone ever *choose* to reason badly? I very much doubt it—though perhaps cases of *akrasia* can be so understood (though even here, there's a *reason* for the shoddy reasoning). In any case, bad reasoning—irrationality—can hardly be the peg upon which to hang a case for libertarian freedom. I'd argue, rather, that we exercise freedom to just the extent that we possess and employ well the rational faculties required for responsible action. To the extent that someone suffers from entrenched irrationality, to that extent we are inclined to offer causal explanations for their thought and behavior, and to withdraw blame.

---

[6]See Evan Fales, "Divine Freedom and the Choice of a World," *International Journal for Philosophy of Religion* 35 (1994): 65-88.

A Naturalist Moral Nonrealism Response

Michael Ruse

I CONFESS TO DEEP FEELINGS OF INADEQUACY in the face of
this paper because I cannot really follow it, and I am quite sure that the
failing is mine rather than the author's. This kind of technical philosophical analysis is simply beyond my ken and ability. This said, in the
spirit of the worst kind of British amateurism, let me have a go at a
number of things that are said in the course of it.

First (and I am not taking these points in the author's order), Yandell
is defending a view he calls moral essentialism. And he does tell us what
he means by that: "Moral essentialism holds that a true moral principle is
necessarily true. It claims that necessary truths are mind-independently
necessary. Thus they are not true in virtue of linguistic convention,
'deep grammar,' the way our mind or brain works, or sociological agreement" (p. 107). So at least we have a starting point there, because I know
that that is not my position! Second, Yandell takes essentialism to be
something that either is or at least could be bound up with God, his
existence and his nature. I have discussed my own thinking on some of
these issues in my response to Mark Linville, so perhaps in a somewhat
cowardly fashion I am going to skip over this here, even though I recognize that the author may well think this the meat of his paper.

Third, Yandell does have some (negative) comments to make about
the sort of thinking of people like me, so I would like to pick up on
these—perhaps more in a sense of clarification, as much as to show that
I am right. I take it that if essentialism is at one end of the spectrum of
analyses of ethics and its truth status (by ethics in this context I presume we mean normative or substantive ethics), then (in Yandell's language) the other end of the spectrum is the "we made it up" end. In
other words, it is mind-dependent and a function of the way that the
mind/brain works. If there are no mind/brains (I am not taking a stand
on the relationship between the two or if indeed they are two), then
there is no ethics.

Now since the author keeps his criticisms at the "relativism is wrong" level of discussion, I will focus in on that. My position, as I explain in my paper, is that (substantive) ethics is no more and no less than the product of natural selection. Those of our would-be ancestors who had ethical feelings survived and reproduced, and those who did not did not. So if we are going to use terms like *objective* and *subjective*, I take it that the Darwinian (me) is very much a subjectivist—no humans, no ethics—whereas the essentialist is very much an objectivist: ethics would still be around and true even if there never had been and never would be any humans (or human-like creatures) at all. Even if there is no one around in the wood, it would still be wrong to shove an unsuspecting victim under a falling tree. But does this plunge someone like me into relativism and hence subject to the author's critical scorn? I don't think that because one is a subjectivist that relativism follows always at once. I think one could be a subjectivist in the way I am and yet not be a relativist at all about something like mathematics. Indeed, in my response to Linville I attempt to explain why I cannot imagine any rational being (at least a rational being as I understand it) refusing to accept $2 + 2 = 4$ and refusing to reject $2 + 2 = 5$. As it happens, I myself am inclined to Platonism about mathematics, so perhaps I am an essentialist here. But I don't think it is silly to be an empiricist and think it is all constructed or some such thing. Without human beings there would be no mathematics. So at least in principle, although a potential subjectivist, I am certainly no relativist in this respect.

But is ethics different? Darwin at some level certainly thought it was. It may be well first to premise that I do not wish to maintain that any strictly social animal, if its intellectual faculties were to become as active and as highly developed as in man, would acquire exactly the same moral sense as ours. In the same manner as various animals have some sense of beauty, though they admire widely different objects, so they might have a sense of right and wrong, though led by it to follow widely different lines of conduct. If, for instance, to take an extreme case, humans were reared under precisely the same conditions as hive bees, there can hardly be a doubt that our unmarried females would, like the worker bees, think it a sacred duty to kill their brothers, and mothers would strive to kill their fertile daughters, and no one would think of interfering. Nevertheless the bee, or any other social animal, would in our supposed case gain, as it appears to me, some feeling of right and wrong, or a conscience.[1]

I think Darwin is right here, so at some level I freely admit to being a relativist. But does this mean that on my own terms I (and Darwin) have values that are "no more 'valid' than those of a child molester" (p. 100)? I sincerely hope not, and if my position (I will speak for Darwin only as much as he would want) implies that then it is certainly wrong. My values have no more objective foundation than those of the child molester (I am assuming that the molester really thinks it is okay to have sex with kids and is not someone who shares my values but who breaks them and sins), but in some real sense of "valid" I think my values more valid.

Note for a start that relativism, if such there be, is intergalactic. Here on this earth, we humans all come from one stock—if truth be known, a very small stock not that long ago. We don't have humanoids around that are bee-like and killing siblings in the name of morality. So in a way the relativism of the Darwinian is a bit hypothetical, or irrelevant at least. For note that morality is a bit like language. It is a shared phenomenon. I might speak far better English than you, but if none of you can understand my accent, it is worthless. Morality—meaning substantive ethics—has to be a shared phenomenon, otherwise it doesn't work. If I think killing babies is a bad thing but no one shares my views, then it doesn't help me much not to have killed your kid when I had the chance if you kill mine as soon as possible. So, recognizing that there are going to be cultural differences—which of course the essentialist has to recognize too—the Darwinian is no relativist on this earth of ours with respect to this species of ours.

But isn't it all just a question of feelings? A bit like the logical positivist view of ethics? I might not like or approve of sex with children, but those are my feelings, and the pedophiliac has his views that are different. I might be able to impose my views by force, but that is all

---

[1]Charles Darwin, *The Descent of Man, and Selection in Relation to Sex* (London: John Murray, 1871).

there is to it. Not quite. It is true that they are all feelings, but note that for the Darwinian the feelings of morality are different from simple feelings of like and dislike—I like spinach, you don't. The feelings of morality have the phenomenological character of being absolute, if you like objective, norms of behavior. For the Darwinian this is no add-on to avoid philosophical controversy, but an essential element of the game. If there were no such "objectification," as John Mackie used to call it, then morality would break down because everyone would ignore it. As it is, we may ignore it, but we do it only at the cost of doing something we feel—we apprehend as—wrong. Really and truly objectively wrong.

So, within the system, we do have our standards, and the pedophiliac fails them and is judged invalid, to use the term we came in with. You may say that that is not enough. But that is the point. That is all the Darwinian can or will give you. But notice that the Darwinian is giving you a real sense of right and wrong, however based—or as I would say, not based. The pedophiliac is either aware of right and wrong like the rest of us but does what is wrong nevertheless, or the pedophiliac is someone with a perverted moral sense. They are a freak of nature as much as someone born with a genetic handicap. Except in their case they are dangerous, and we must act against them to save the rest of us.

But isn't it still possible that certain situations trigger moral emotions that go against the norm? What about the Russian soldiers raping all of those German women in the last year of the war? Wasn't that natural in some sense, at least natural within the context of a theory like Darwinism that puts such a premium on reproduction? Actually, not necessarily. I personally find nothing amiss with saying every one of those Russians was doing the wrong thing. We know why they did it. Sex is enjoyable. They hated the Germans. They could get away with it. But that doesn't make it right. A lot of us cheat on our income tax, calculating that we can get away with it, but it doesn't make it right.

But if you persist and throw up psychological and sociological evidence that the Russian soldiers were actually thinking they were doing a morally good thing, then I suspect at a pinch the Darwinian can account for the phenomenon (a bit like Darwin's bees), but I wonder whether the essentialist—particularly the Christian essentialist—can do so. We have fully mature, reflective human beings, genuinely thinking that they are doing the morally right thing. They are obeying their version of the categorical imperative, even though it is not Kant's. At the very least, one starts to wonder about how the moral dictates of the essentialist function, if they are hidden from people who really are trying to find and obey them. (You have to put in these qualifying clauses because if you don't then there is no need for the Darwinian to be bound by them either.) For myself I would rather say that it is all a matter of human vagaries than ethereal moral norms.

To come back to where I came in. I am sorry if Keith Yandell thinks that I am simply ignoring his arguments. I suspect he is true. But there are points in his piece where I can see we differ strongly, and so at least in partial mitigation I have tried to address these and show why I prefer my own position.

A Moral Particularism Response

Mark D. Linville

ONE MAY INFER FROM MY OWN ESSAY, "Moral Particularism," that I am in agreement with Professor Yandell on many points. Beyond our shared commitment to Christian theism, we agree that the oft-urged Euthyphro dilemma is not a dilemma after all. There are more options for the theist than allowed on standard versions of the argument, and several of these are explored in Professor Yandell's careful discussion. We agree that voluntarism—the idea that morality hinges on the arbitrary decrees of God—is beset with grave difficulties that should render it unattractive to the theist.[1] We both affirm moral realism, eschewing all varieties of relativism, and allege that there are objectively and necessarily true moral principles—in particular, a principle of respect for persons.

What disagreement there is lies in our differing views regarding the ultimate grounding for morality. Professor Yandell affirms moral essentialism, according to which morality derives from necessarily true propositions—abstract objects—that do not depend for their truth or existence on God or anything else. They are such that they *could not* have been false. Whereas many think that such a view is a threat to divine sovereignty, aseity or omnipotence, Professor Yandell thinks not. If it is impossible, say, that the law of noncontradiction might have been false there appears to be no good sense in which one might say that God "created" it or brought it about that it is true. A Sunday school teacher once assured my two skeptical sons that "God can do anything" and that "anything" includes both existing and not existing—at the same time and in the same respect—if God so chooses. She was mistaken, both in the assertion itself and in the underlying assumption that to say anything less would fetter the Almighty. As C. S. Lewis once

---

[1]Christians who affirm the substitutionary theory of the atonement have, I think, an additional reason to reject voluntarism. If "justice" is whatever God arbitrarily decrees it to be, then, to borrow from the apostle Paul, "Christ died needlessly." There are no objective demands of justice to be satisfied by the cross of Christ.

observed, nonsense remains nonsense even if prefaced with the words "God can." And if *having inherent worth* is an essential property of persons, then God could no more have created persons who were bereft of this property than he could have fashioned triangles the sum of whose interior angles was other than 180 degrees. I argued in my main essay that God values persons because they are valuable, and not the other way around. Still, I suggest that God himself, and neither some independent principle nor God's arbitrary decree, serves as the standard for morals and values. God himself is the Good. As Professor Yandell has described at least some cousin of my view, God's nature serves as "exemplar." Further, created persons have inherent worth in that as creatures bearing the *imago Dei* they bear an important resemblance to the person who is God.

Professor Yandell rightly points out that such a moral exemplar view, together with the belief that there are necessarily true moral propositions, entails God's necessary existence. And he observes that for those, such as myself, who affirm divine necessity, it is "puzzling" why they would not hold some variety of nonvoluntarist (and, presumably, nonessentialist) views. But Professor Yandell is not to be counted among the ranks of Anselmian theists, who ascribe such necessity to God. What he has elsewhere called "plain theism" (PT) suggests that, whatever "logically necessary existence" means, at its core is the commitment to God's necessary causal independence (NCI). On PT, it is a necessary truth that God is without beginning or end, and that he does not depend for his existence upon anything beside himself. But even if God exists *at all times* within each world in which he exists, this does not entail that God exists in "every way a world might be." I take it that Professor Yandell does not think that *God has necessary existence* is demonstrably (and, if so, necessarily) false. Perhaps it is a widely accepted dogma that no existential proposition is necessary, but those who embrace it appear to walk by faith rather than sight. Rather, he thinks that we lack any proof of God's necessary existence, and besides, the important concerns regarding God's aseity and such are satisfied by the concept of a logically contingent but NCI being.

The "lack of proof" claim turns upon his assessment of one version of the ontological argument. Bertrand Russell once tossed his tobacco tin into the air and exclaimed, "Great God in boots! The ontological argument is sound!" I've neither tossed tobacco tins nor said such a thing. Nor have I thought the success of the Anselmian argument necessary for the affirmation of an Anselmian "perfect being" theology. Rather, the concept appears to arise out of common religious experience and the belief that there is a being who is worthy of worship.[2] God is a perfect being in the event that he has all "perfections" or great-making properties, and so much hinges on whether necessary existence is a perfection.[3] An unlikely theologian, J. N. Findlay, asserted that the "demands and claims inherent in religious attitudes" are contrary to the notion that their object should exist "accidentally." He went on to observe that the same convictions call for the *essential* possession of God's various great-making properties.[4] My impression is that many would-be worshipers would view PT as offering a diminished view of the divine nature and less suited as the object of worship. And they might worry over the contingency of God's existence. Chesterton once confessed his concern that God would "drop the cosmos with a crash." What assurances have we from PT that *God himself* might not go tumbling from the heavens and out of existence? The eternal security for the saved is assured only if the same may be said of the Savior.[5] Whatever may be said of such motivation for perfect-being theology and its ascription of NCI to God, the plain theist too is motivated by a concern to have a sufficiently exalted view of God. Presumably, the ascription of NCI to God is out of a concern for divine aseity. And careful formula-

---

[2]"Conceiving of God as a perfect being need not require starting with the Ontological Argument: the idea may also grow out of reflection on religious experience" (Edward Wierenga, *The Nature of God* [Ithaca, N.Y.: Cornell University Press, 1989], p. 5).

[3]On the face of it, to suggest that *existence* is among God's essential attributes says little to set him apart from you, me or a teapot. If God is essentially omniscient, then God is omniscient in all worlds in which God exists. But if God "has existence" essentially, then God exists in every world in which God exists. So it is for the teapot. But to say that God has *necessary* existence essentially is to say that, in each world in which God exists, God has the property of existing in *all* possible worlds. Most teapots fall short on this count.

[4]Wierenga, *Nature of God*, p. 3.

[5]Presumably, we shall be told that God's attributes—e.g., goodness, omnipotence, omniscience—in the actual world will cooperate to ensure the perpetuation of God's existence. Whether a successful case can be made out for this is a question for another discussion.

tions of such attributes as omnipotence, as we find in Professor Yandell's essay, are likely underdetermined by specific biblical teachings but are motivated by a concern to preserve a sufficiently robust concept of God. One issue, then, between the Anselmian and the plain theist is over whether necessary existence is required for a sufficiently high view of God. Beyond all of this, even if divine necessity is not established through a sound ontological or cosmological argument, it emerges as the conclusion of a reversal of Professor Yandell's argument: If morality depends upon God, then God exists necessarily; morality depends upon God; therefore, God exists necessarily.[6] As it is said, one person's *modus tollens* is another person's *modus ponens*.

In what remains, I want to address Professor Yandell's closing suggestion that moral essentialism should be "attractive and open to both theists and nontheists." Perhaps he is correct in his assertion that having morality grounded in necessarily and independently existing abstracta is not a threat to theistic belief. Is such a view a viable option for naturalists such as Ruse and Fales? I think the combination of metaphysical naturalism with moral essentialism forms an unstable compound. So did George Santayana, who argued Bertrand Russell out of his early affirmation of moral realism.[7] On the one hand, according to Santayana, Russell's view implied, "In the realm of essences, before anything exists, there are certain essences that have this remarkable property, that they ought to exist, or at least, that, if anything exists, it ought to conform to them."[8]

On the other hand, given Russell's naturalism, "What exists . . . is deaf to this moral emphasis in the eternal; nature exists for no reason."[9] As Russell famously put it, "Man is the product of causes that had no

---

[6]God's moral perfection must also be a matter of necessity on the view I defend. To imagine a possible world in which God sins is to imagine a world in which God and the moral standard part company. But if it is possible that the moral standard is distinct from God, then the two are *necessarily* distinct.

[7]For a more extensive consideration of Santayana's interesting arguments, see Mark D. Linville, "Why Bertrand Russell Was Not a Moral Realist, Either" in *Philosophy and the Christian Worldview: Analysis, Assessment and Development*, ed. David Werther and Mark D. Linville (London: Continuum Books, 2012), pp. 157-74.

[8]George Santayana, *Winds of Doctrine* and *Platonism and the Spiritual Life* (New York: Harper, 1957), p. 153.

[9]Ibid.

prevision of the end they were achieving."[10] But in such an accidental world it would be marvelous indeed if the very things that *ought* to exist should have come to be. It would be as though among the verities a special premium had forever been placed upon something—moral agents, say—and, despite the countless possibilities and, because of sheer dumb luck, the same had been fashioned and formed of big bang debris. Further, if human hopes and fears, loves and beliefs are, as Russell affirmed, "but the outcome of accidental collocations of atoms," or, perhaps more to the point, the product of natural selection, it would be especially surprising to learn that, by fortuitous circumstance and with no direction or influence from any heaven above, the emergent human conscience, to which Russell appeals, is a reliable indicator of eternal moral truth. Russell observes a bit later in "A Free Man's Worship" that it is a "strange mystery" that nature, "omnipotent but blind" should, in her "secular hurrying," have "brought forth at last a child, subject still to her power, but gifted with sight, with knowledge of good and evil, with the capacity of judging all the works of his unthinking mother." It would be a strange mystery indeed if, as Darwin imagined and both Ruse and Fales have mentioned, there are all sorts of human "moralities" that *might* have been had the circumstances of evolution been relevantly different. Darwin's example is of people—or moral agents of some sort—being reared in the same conditions as hive bees. In that event, conscience would have urged the acts of infanticide and siblicide as "sacred duties." Presumably, Professor Yandell's moral essentialism would have it that there are necessarily true propositions regarding the wrongness of such acts. But in light of these Darwinian possibilities it would be astonishing to suppose that the contingencies of the evolutionary landscape just happened to be such that the emergent human conscience is such that our moral beliefs generally get things right. As Santayana saw it, what was missing from Russell's metaphysics but provided on theism—including Plato's brand of theism—was any account of how the Good might influence the course of nature.

---

[10]Bertrand Russell, *Why I Am Not a Christian: And Other Essays on Religion and Related Subjects* (New York: Simon & Schuster, 1957), p. 107.

The whole Platonic and Christian scheme, in making the good independent of private will and opinion, by no means makes it independent of the direction of nature in general and of human nature in particular. For all things have been created with an innate predisposition towards the creative good and are capable of finding happiness in nothing else. Obligation, in this system, remains internal and vital. Plato attributes a single vital direction and a single narrow source to the cosmos. This is what determines and narrows the source of the true good; for the true good is that relevant to nature. Plato would not have been a dogmatic moralist had he not been a theist.[11]

Note that this concern is indifferent between Professor Yandell's account and mine regarding God's nature and relation to morality.[12] While I have defended the idea that God himself serves as the moral exemplar, this is not necessary for providing the metaphysical underpinnings that seem to be lacking. If Professor Yandell is right, both God and the relevant abstract objects exist. Though morality is not derived from God's commands or nature, God is available to bring it about that nature and human nature are alive to the verities of heaven.

---

[11]Santayana, *Winds of Doctrine*, p. 143n.

[12]And I think I should allow that *any* metaphysic that sees the natural world as having been shaped—either directly or indirectly—by such a moral realm would have a proposed solution to this problem. John Leslie's *Infinite Minds* (Oxford: Clarendon Press, 2001), for instance, urges the idea that what exists is explained by reference to its *value*—without any essential reference to a personal creator or demiurge

4

Moral Particularism

Mark D. Linville

Bertrand Russell was not a Christian, and he took the trouble to say why he was not. Among other things, he was of the opinion that none of the proposed arguments for God's existence really works. And among these are varieties of "moral arguments for deity," some of which argue that "there would be no right or wrong unless God existed." Russell makes short work of this suggestion:

> I am not for the moment concerned with whether there is a difference between right and wrong, or whether there is not: that is another question. The point I am concerned with is that, if you are quite sure there is a difference between right and wrong, then you are in this situation: Is that difference due to God's fiat or is it not? If it is due to God's fiat, then for God himself there is no difference between right and wrong, and it is no longer a significant statement to say that God is good. If you are going to say, as theologians do, that God is good, you must then say that right and wrong have some meaning which is independent of God's fiat, because God's fiats are good and not bad independently of the mere fact that he made them. If you are going to say that, you will then have to say that it is not only through God that right and wrong came into being, but that they are in their essence logically anterior to God.[1]

At one time, Russell himself had been "quite sure there is a difference between right and wrong." In his early essay, "The Elements of

---

[1]Bertrand Russell, *Why I Am Not a Christian* (New York: Touchstone Books, 1967), p. 12.

Ethics," he had affirmed perhaps as clear a statement of moral realism as has ever been formulated: "The object of ethics, by its own account, is to discover true propositions about virtuous and vicious conduct, and . . . these are just as much a part of truth as true propositions about oxygen or the multiplication table."[2] By the time he wrote *Why I Am Not a Christian* he had abandoned that conviction. Ironically, the arguments responsible for that abandonment might be pressed into the service of the sort of moral argument that he here criticizes.[3] The present essay assumes the same moral realism that was defended by the early Russell, but aims to present a model for thinking of objective morals as being ultimately dependent on God. Our question, then, is whether the proponent of the moral argument is, indeed, in the "situation" that Russell suggests.

A CRITIQUE OF MORALITY BY DIVINE FIAT

Russell appears to have the classic Euthyphro dilemma in mind. At Euthyphro's suggestion that piety is "whatever the gods love," Socrates asked, "Is piety pious because the gods love it, or do the gods love it because it is pious?" In exploration of the first horn of that dilemma, Russell considers the suggestion that the difference between right and wrong is due to God's "fiat," or creative activity, so that moral distinctions were conjured from the amoral void. Given such a view of things, we might imagine Moses descending Sinai, tablets in arm, with breaking news for the Israelites waiting breathlessly below: "Hey, everyone! It's '*not*'! 'Thou shalt *not* commit adultery!'" After all, if the distinction between right and wrong is due to divine fiat in the way that Russell has in mind, things might well have gone either way.

This sort of view is not without its advocates. Consider, for instance,

---

[2]Bertrand Russell, "The Elements of Ethics," *Philosophical Essays* (1910; reprint, London: Routledge, 1994), p. 13.

[3]George Santayana's arguments appear to have been the catalyst for this change in belief. For a discussion of Santayana's critique of Russell's early "hypostatic ethics," see Mark D. Linville, "Why Bertrand Russell Was Not a Moral Realist, Either," in *Philosophy and the Christian Worldview: Analysis, Assessment and Development*, ed. David Werther and Mark D. Linville (New York: Continuum Books, forthcoming).

William of Ockham's striking suggestion regarding the relationship between God and morality.

> The hatred of God, theft, adultery, and actions similar to these actions according to the common law, may have an evil quality *annexed*, insofar as they are done by someone who is obligated by a divine command to perform the opposite act. But as far as the *sheer being* in these actions is concerned, they can be performed by God without any evil condition annexed; and they can even be performed meritoriously by an earthly pilgrim if they should come under a divine precept, just as now the opposite of these in fact fall under a divine command.[4]

The language is instructive. Adultery, for example, has an evil quality "annexed"—added on—only insofar as there is an actual divine prohibition against it. But so far as the "sheer being" of the acts are concerned, adultery and fidelity, theft and honesty, hatred and love are all moral—or, more accurately, *amoral*—equivalents, with equal potential for being the Father's business. The view, then, is that moral properties are not inherent and essential to acts. Rather, they are *relational* and contingent. Determining the moral properties of an act is, for God, a little like painting a barn. Even though the Ten Commandments *were*, as a matter of fact, written in stone, they are in principle subject to revision: "Ye have heard that it was said by them of old time, 'Thou shalt not commit adultery.' But I say unto you, *Copulo ergo sum!*"[5]

Now, Russell argues that if *this* is one's view of the nature of moral properties, then "for God himself there is no difference between right and wrong." Presumably, God is no more subject to moral laws of his own devising than he is to the physical laws and regularities that he has put into place. One consequence here is that one can no longer meaningfully say that God is *good*, morally speaking. For on this view, an act is right or a person good insofar as they do what God wills or commands. Of course, it is always true that God does as God wills,

---

[4]William of Ockham, *On the Four Books of the Sentences* 2, 19, in *Divine Command Morality*, ed. Janine Marie Idziak (New York: Edwin Mellen, 1979), pp. 56-57.

[5]The phrase was, I think, first formulated by Malcolm Muggeridge in an essay critiquing his culture's obsession with sex.

and, presumably, he practices what he preaches. But, taken alone, this observation seems unhelpful. Satan does as Satan wills, but this hardly inspires admiration, let alone adoration. What we wish to know is whether what God wills and does is *right* and whether he is *good* for doing it, and the judgment that he is such appears to require some independent standard in virtue of which we might offer that assessment. But then Russell observes that the discovery of such a principle leads us to conclude that moral distinctions are "logically anterior to God," so that when God pronounced his creation "good" this was merely the recognition of values already in place rather than their *ex nihilo* creation.

One might reply that we have not understood the full import of the view if we persist in asking such questions. After all, the claim is that moral rightness *just is* a matter of an act's being either prescribed or performed by God. John Duns Scotus insisted, "From the fact that something is suitable to the divine will, it is right; and whatever action God could perform is right absolutely." He added that the *justice* of God is "coextensive with" the *power* of God, with the result that "justice in God also extends to opposites."[6] Thus, the right-making property here is just the property *being performed by God*, so that this property is necessarily sufficient for rightness. To insist that one has yet to be told whether God is good or his acts right is thus to beg the question against the view being affirmed.

There is, I think, something in this reply. Scotus identified the will of God as the "first principle of righteousness," and some of the apparent trouble may have simply to do with the logic of such first principles or ultimate standards. Suppose that a meter is determined by the length of an actual platinum bar housed in Paris. A rattlesnake is one meter long just in case it is the same length as the bar. Is the bar also a meter long? Well, the bar is the same length as itself.

A fundamental question of normative ethics is, What *makes* right acts right and wrong acts wrong? Competing ethical theories differ among themselves in various ways, but a chief difference is in their re-

---

6John Duns Scotus, *The Paris Commentary on the Sentences*, bk. 4, chap. 46, in Idziak, ed., *Divine Command Morality*, p. 54.

spective answers to this question. And this question is typically answered by appeal to whatever is taken to be the first principle of morality. I might maintain, for instance, that a right act is one that treats persons with respect, and a wrong act is one that treats persons with disrespect. Here, *being respectful* and *being disrespectful* are the right-making and wrong-making properties of acts. Suppose you ask me, "Is it morally right to act in accordance with the principle of respect for persons?" or "Is the principle of respect for persons a morally good principle?" Since I take this as the first principle of morality, I can hardly answer by showing how it is endorsed by some *higher* moral authority. Indeed, were I to appeal to such a higher court, then I would demonstrate that I was not regarding respect for persons as a *first principle* after all, and you would be free to raise the same question regarding whatever I offered as that higher principle. At one level, then, about all I can say in answer to your question is that acting in accordance with the principle of respect for persons is prescribed by the principle of respect for persons and is therefore right. And it is a morally good principle in that it is perfectly consistent with the first principle of morality—which also happens to be itself.[7] Perhaps, then, the apparent circularity and vacuity that arise from positing the divine will as a first principle have less to do with the "divine will" part than with the bit about its being a first principle.

But I do believe that Russell's critique succeeds in the end. Consider Duns Scotus's suggestion that "the justice of God extends to opposites" and Ockham's suggestion that any two "moral opposites" are equally "right" or "good" as long as they stand in the right relation to some divine command. In the case of God himself, if God creates Adam, surrounds him with the requirements for human flourishing, pays frequent calls, extends health and retirement benefits, and seeks eternal fellowship and friendship with him, then God is said to be "good." And if God breathes life into Adam, who, upon waking, experiences nothing but exquisite pain, confusion, torment and grief, all of which last for all eternity, then God is likewise said to be "good." As the Calvinist

---

[7]On the other hand, I may seek to answer your question by considering the implications of the principle if followed consistently and the plausibility of its account of right-making properties.

theologian Gordon Clark once put it, "Anything God does is right, because he does it."[8] But on such an account we seem to have lost sight of any meaningful content to the term. Like any term whatsoever—moral or nonmoral—it is meaningful only if it picks out some things and not others.

Suppose you hear me using a new word: *bleen*. At first you've no idea what this means, but you scrutinize the context of use in order to determine my meaning. You note that I refer to the carpet, which has a sort of blue-green color, as "bleen." You conclude that this is my eccentric way of saying "bluish green." But then I use it to refer to a lampshade that is fire-engine red, an unseen dog barking in the night, a Mozart piano concerto, unicorns, my kind Aunt Nina, the wicked wizard Gargamel, plate tectonics, and a bowl of oatmeal with raisins. The weather is always bleen regardless of conditions. Sometimes it seems clear that I like or approve of the bleen thing; other times not. And *bleen* makes appearances variously as noun, verb, adverb (*bleenly*) or adjective without rhyme or reason. In this case you've no clue what I mean by *bleen*. Nor do I. Terms that are indifferent in their application are vacuous. Moral terms that are morally indifferent in their application are morally vacuous. Gottfried Leibniz expressed a related concern over the suggestion that "the works of God are good only through the formal reason that God has made them."

> In saying, therefore, that things are not good according to any standard of goodness, but simply by the will of God, it seems to me that one destroys, without realizing it, all the love of God and all his glory; for why praise him for what he has done, if he would be equally praiseworthy in doing the contrary? Where will be his justice and his wisdom if he has only a certain despotic power, if arbitrary will takes the place of reasonableness, and if in accord with the definition of tyrants, justice consists in that which is pleasing to the most powerful?[9]

---

[8]Gordon Clark, *Religion Reason and Revelation* (Nutley, N.J.: Craig Press, 1961), p. 185.
[9]Gottfried W. Leibniz, *Discourse on Metaphysics and Other Essays*, trans. Daniel Garber and Roger Ariew (Indianapolis: Hackett, 1991), p. 2.

In saying, "Though he slay me yet shall I trust in him," Job was not, I think, expressing a determination to acquiesce in the experiments of a sadistic cosmic torturer. Nor do I think he was suggesting that God is to be "trusted" even if he is not, in fact, trustworthy. *Trust*, too, would be meaningless apart from some fixed and substantive notion of what is good, plus the conviction that the object of that trust is both willing and able to bring about that good. It is one thing to trust, with Job, that God is good despite present appearances; it is quite another to reconcile oneself to the suggestion that God is "good" regardless of what God is like.[10] John Stuart Mill once proclaimed, "I will call no being good, who is not what I mean when I apply that epithet to my fellow-creatures; and if such a being can sentence me to hell for not so calling him, to hell I will go."[11] In assessing Mill's view, the Christian apologist E. J. Carnell characterized this as an "outburst against the Almighty" and invoked a Psalm: "He that sits in the heavens will laugh: the Lord will have them in derision (Psalm 2:4)."[12] At the risk of that same divine derision, I side with Mill. And I have the company of another Christian apologist. C. S. Lewis noted that "if God's moral judgement differs from ours so that our 'black' may be His 'white', we can mean nothing by calling Him good." In that case, saying, "God is good" amounts to saying "God is *I know not what*." He added, "If He is not (in our sense) 'good' we shall obey, if at all, only through fear—and should be equally ready to obey an omnipotent Fiend."[13] In this case, it is hard

---

[10]Normally, we suppose that one's *moral* properties are intimately related to whatever nonmoral or "natural" properties they display. I think that Hitler was *depraved*. Ask me why, and I will cite a list of his nonmoral properties: His anti-Semitism, his will to power, monomania, indifference to human suffering and the value of human life, and so on. I might say, then, that Hitler's depravity is *constituted* by some such set of nonmoral properties, P1, P2, P3 and P4. Suppose you observe that, say, Stalin displayed *precisely* the same set of properties, P1, P2, P3 and P4, and note that he too must have been depraved. You would be puzzled if I agreed that the two were exactly alike in their relevant nonmoral properties, but that, while Hitler was morally depraved, Stalin was a moral saint. We appear to have the same sort of disconnect here between God's alleged moral property of goodness and whatever nonmoral description holds true of God and his actions. It is as if we were to insist that Hitler would have been "depraved" even had he grown to be the kindest of men with love in his heart, good will for his fellow man, and his own children's show *Mr. Schicklgruber's Neighborhood*.

[11]J. S. Mill, *An Examination of Sir William Hamilton's Philosophy* (London: Longmans Green, 1865), p. 131.

[12]E. J. Carnell, *An Introduction to Christian Apologetics* (Grand Rapids: Eerdmans, 1948), p. 307.

[13]C. S. Lewis, *The Problem of Pain* (New York: Harper Collins, 2001), p. 29.

to see how to resist the Kantian assessment that "any system of morals erected on this foundation would be directly opposed to morality."[14]

WHAT EUTHYPHRO MIGHT HAVE SAID

Russell is right. There are deep problems for the theist who maintains that morality is ultimately the product of divine fiat. He seems, however, to assume that such must be the position of any theist who maintains that "there would be no right or wrong unless God existed." But why think this? It seems to me that there are more plausible options available to the theist. A mainstream position in the history of theology has it that *God himself*—and not God's arbitrary commands—serves as the ultimate criterion. Thomas Aquinas, for instance, held that God is good not in the sense that he *participates* in some criterion distinct from and prior to himself, but in that God is *goodness* itself.

> God is . . . goodness itself, and not only good. . . . The perfection of the divine being is not affirmed on the basis of something added to it, but because the divine being, as was shown above, is perfect in itself. The goodness of God, therefore, is not something added to his substance; his substance is his goodness.[15]

Aquinas's view regarding God's relationship to moral goodness is an application of his broader doctrine of divine simplicity. That view denies that God *has* a nature constituted of various attributes. Rather, God is *identical* to his nature. Thus God is "goodness itself." But he is also identical to his omnipotence, omniscience and omnipresence. And on one plausible reading of this doctrine, God's goodness is identical to his omnipotence, his omnipotence to his omniscience, and so on. These are hard sayings. For one thing, at least on the face of it, these properties *seem* to be distinct features of anything that has them. For another, as Alvin Plantinga has argued, if God is identical to some property, such as goodness, then God is a property.[16] But no property

---

[14]Immanuel Kant, *Groundwork of the Metaphysics of Morals* 443, trans. H. J. Paton (New York: Harper Torchbooks, 1964), p. 110.

[15]Thomas Aquinas, *Summa Contra Gentiles* 1.38.2-3, trans. Anton Pegis (South Bend, Ind.: University of Notre Dame Press, 1975), p. 153.

[16]Alvin Plantinga, *Does God Have a Nature?* (Milwaukee: Marquette University Press, 1980).

is a person, and so God is not a person. This news will come as a surprise to many.

Perhaps there is a way of resolving these apparent problems with Aquinas's doctrine. The present point is neither to criticize nor defend the doctrine of simplicity itself, but to note the turn to God's necessary nature, as opposed to the contingencies of an arbitrary will, as the standard. If anything like Aquinas's view is defensible, then we may be afforded the makings of a reply to Russell. It will be true that "there would be no right or wrong unless God existed," but, in this case, morality would be neither by divine fiat nor would it have its roots in foreign soil, so to speak.

I think the general move to God himself as the standard holds some promise in light of the traditional Euthyphro objection. The outlines of such a position were suggested by William Alston in an essay titled "What Euthyphro Should Have Said" and developed further in "Some Suggestions for Divine Command Theorists."[17] According to Alston, while the view he develops has some affinities with that of Aquinas, in that the two views arrive at "approximately the same destination," there is no commitment to the Thomistic doctrine of divine simplicity. That shared destination is the claim that *God himself* is the ultimate criterion of value. Alston refers to this feature of his view as "value particularism," since the criterion of value is a particular being rather than a principle or abstract idea. However, he does not think that appeal to God or God's nature is of itself sufficient for distinguishing goodness in general from moral *obligation* or duty. After all, it is implausible to suppose that we are morally obligated to do anything and everything that it would be good for us to do. Perhaps it would be good of me to spend a part of my day baking cookies to share with my neighbors, but I do not think it is *wrong* of me to refrain. On Alston's view, then, though God himself is the criterion of *value*, God's commands are the source of *moral obligation*. And so, he defends a variety

[17]William Alston, "What Euthyphro Should Have Said," in *Philosophy of Religion: A Reader and Guide*, ed. William Lane Craig (New Brunswick, N.J.: Rutgers University Press, 2002), pp. 283-98; "Some Suggestions for Divine Command Theorists," in William Alston, *Divine Nature and Human Language: Essays in Philosophical Theology* (Ithaca, N.Y.: Cornell University Press, 1989), pp. 253-74.

of divine command morality that is tempered with discussion of the role of the divine nature. While I find the appeal to God's nature promising, I am not convinced that moral obligation should be conceived as being constituted by divine commands. In the final section I will offer suggestions toward the construction of what I call *moral particularism*: the idea that God's nature serves as the standard for moral rightness as well as goodness.

Alston's purpose is thus to suggest "what view of God and human morality a divine command theorist should adopt if she is to be in the best position to deal with [the Euthyphro] dilemma."[18]

He begins by setting out a central claim of divine command morality:

(1) Divine commands are constitutive of moral obligation.

Here, we are not offered a theory regarding the *meaning* of any moral term, such as *right* or *wrong*. The suggestion is not that "moral obligation" and "divine command" are synonymous and interchangeable. It is not an analysis of such moral concepts as obligation, rightness or wrongness—no more than *Gold is that element of the atomic number of 79* is an account of what people *mean* when they speak of "gold." People understood that *All is not golde that glystereth* long before any talk of periodic tables. Gold *just is* the element whose nucleus contains 79 protons, and we've no reason to question this identity simply because one may meaningfully ask, "I *know* the stuff in them thar hills has 79 protons in its nucleus, *but is it gold*?" In the same way, Alston suggests that the property of *being morally obligatory* is either identical to or supervenient upon the property *being commanded by God*. It will hardly do, then, to observe that people seldom have either God or his commands in view when they think themselves morally obligated to do a thing.

Nor does Alston's view imply that knowledge of right and wrong presupposes any knowledge of theology or even belief in God. It is thus impervious to the common objection that one need not believe in God in order to see that, say, spousal abuse or recreational baby-stomping

---

[18]Alston, "What Euthyphro Should Have Said," p. 283.

are wrong.[19] In fact, as Alston himself observes, the view has no such epistemological implications whatever.

> The particularist is free to recognize that God has so constructed us and our environment that we are led to form sound value judgments under various circumstances without tracing them back to the ultimate standard.[20]

In fact, it is not clear to me that there is a necessary connection between Alston's particularism and *any* specific view of moral epistemology. It does entail that *whichever* faculties are rightly employed in the acquisition of moral knowledge have been endowed by the Creator, but whether this involves, for instance, rational inferences, sense perception or some combination is, I think, to be settled only after careful work in epistemology and moral philosophy. My own view is that certain of our moral beliefs, such as the belief that kindness is better than cruelty or that people ought not to be treated as mere things, have their warrant not as inferences from more basic or certainly known premises, but as the products of moral faculties in good working order.

The mad scientist is both a scientist and mad. Though he is mad, he may nevertheless have method, and it may be unquestionably scientific. The trouble is not in his reason but in his starting assumption that he is Theodore Roosevelt and is charged with the construction of the Natural History Museum. He may, in fact, assemble a fine collection. If I am convinced that I am a brain in a vat, and the subject of that mad scientist's experiments, there is no evidence or argument that will persuade me otherwise. You and your arguments are part of the hallucination that he is creating. This is why Chesterton said that curing a madman is not to argue with a philosopher but to cast out a devil. It is similarly possible to be both an eminent logician and a notorious scoundrel. Moral lapses are not typically lapses of reason but a failure to

---

[19]The typical claim made by the proponent of the moral argument for God's existence is that theism is in a better position to account for the existence of moral properties or facts than is naturalism. This is commonly misheard by critics as the suggestion that atheists and other nontheists are not or cannot be virtuous or recognize virtues when they see them. One might as well take the mind-body dualist, who argues that consciousness remains unexplained unless there is an immaterial mind, to be asserting that all physicalists are zombies.

[20]Alston, *Divine Nature and Human Language*, p. 271.

recognize what Thomas Reid referred to as first principles.

> It is a first principle in morals, That we ought not do to another what
> we should think wrong to be done to us in like circumstances. If a
> man is not capable of perceiving this in his cool moments, when he
> reflects seriously, he is not a moral agent, nor is he capable of being
> convinced of it by reasoning.[21]

I am unaware of any premises more certainly known than the proposition *Recreational baby-stomping is wrong.* I find that I believe it as
soon as I entertain it, and so I believe it as basic. Nevertheless, I think
the belief is warranted, and it is a belief shared by all persons who entertain it and whose relevant faculties are functioning properly. And
the point is relevant to our discussion for two reasons. First, we've no
reason to suppose that a lack of theistic belief entails a lack of properly
functioning moral faculties. Second, it may nevertheless be true that
the theist is in a better position than is, say, the naturalist to explain
how the human species may have come to possess faculties that are
reliable indicators of moral truth. For, as Alston has suggested, the
theist will hold that such faculties have been specifically designed with
that task in mind.[22]

What then ought Euthyphro to have said? Are right acts right because God commands them, or does God command them because they
are right? Pretty clearly, the first horn is implied by (1). But, as we have
seen, to embrace that horn seems to imply that God's commands are
morally arbitrary, and it also appears to leave the divine command theorist with no meaningful way of saying that God is morally good. Indeed, suppose we accept

(1) Divine commands are constitutive of moral obligation.

If this is so, then one fulfills one's moral obligations by obeying divine commands. Suppose that we also accept

---

[21]Thomas Reid, *Inquiry and Essays*, ed. Ronald E. Beanblossom and Keith Lehrer (Indianapolis:
Hackett, 1983), p. 321.
[22]I develop an argument along these lines in my essay "The Moral Argument," in *The Blackwell
Companion to Natural Theology*, ed. J. P. Moreland and William Lane Craig (Oxford: Blackwell, 2009).

(2) God is good insofar as God fulfills his moral obligations.

Then it appears that we inherit an albatross:

(3) God is good insofar as God obeys divine commands.

The trouble is that (3)—or something like it—follows from (1) and (2), and the divine command theorist is essentially committed to (1). Alston's strategy, then, is to reject (2). God's goodness is not a matter of God's fulfilling his moral obligations. There is good reason for this. God *hasn't any* moral obligations.

> However, (1) implies that divine moral goodness is a matter of obeying divine commands only if moral obligation attaches to God; and I take it that the divine command theorist's best move is to deny just this. If the kind(s) of moral status that are engendered by divine commands are attributable only to creatures, then no puzzles can arise over the constitution of divine morality by divine commands.[23]

As we have seen, William of Ockham suggested that God can do absolutely *anything* "without any evil condition annexed," and so this is one way of denying that "moral obligation attaches to God." But is there any good sense in which we may say that God is *morally* good despite not having—and therefore not *meeting*—any moral obligations? The crux of Alston's discussion is found in a twofold claim: (a) God is *essentially* perfectly good—in a way that includes *moral* goodness—and (b) moral obligations do not apply to an essentially perfectly good being.

To say that God is essentially perfectly good is to say that God's perfect goodness is among his essential properties or kind-defining attributes, along with his omnipotence and omnipotence. As Alston has it, "If God is essentially perfectly good . . . it is, in the strongest possible way, impossible for God to fail to do what is right."[24] Again, "If God is essentially perfectly good, then it is metaphysically impossible that God should do anything that is less than supremely good; and this in-

---

[23]Alston, "What Euthyphro Should Have Said," p. 286.
[24]Alston, *Divine Nature and Human Language*, p. 256.

cludes the moral good as well as other modes of goodness."[25] On this view, it is not merely the case that God has so far managed to navigate the straight and narrow. Rather, it is that he *cannot* sin.[26] Indeed, there is *no possible world* in which God exists and misses the mark. Such a view has an important consequence for the divine command theorist, for it implies that it is impossible for him either to commit or to command wrongful acts. What God commands will accord with his essential nature as a perfect being. Where Ockham imagines a time or a possible world in which "the hatred of God, theft, adultery and actions similar to these" may "come under a divine precept," such commands are precluded if God is essentially good. "Since he is perfectly good by nature, it is impossible that God should command us to act in ways that are not for the best."[27] But what if God *were* to issue the sorts of commands that Ockham imagines? Would it then be our duty to curse God, steal coveted power tools from our neighbors and run off to Tahiti with their spouses? The answer is that, since on the view under consideration such commands are an impossibility for God, it is a little like asking, If the wheels on pickup trucks were square circles would they handle well in snow? or How many doughnuts would come in a dozen if seven plus five made thirteen?

The claim, then, is that God is essentially perfectly good, but Alston argues that the divine goodness is not to be construed in terms of the fulfillment of moral obligations. Here, he takes his cue from Immanuel Kant. According to Kant, God is a being whose nature "necessarily conforms to objective law" and "whose maxims necessarily are in harmony with the laws of autonomy" because his will is "incapable of any maxims which conflict with the moral law."[28] God's will manifests an "irrefragable agreement . . . with the pure moral law" so that such

---

[25]Ibid., p. 257.

[26]Religious believers may balk at the suggestion that God *cannot* (i.e., is *unable to*) do this or that. But there appears to be biblical ground for this. Paul writes in Titus 1:2 (KJV) that God *cannot* lie. The author of Hebrews (6:18) claims that it is *impossible* for God to lie. James 1:13 asserts that God *cannot* be tempted (and, in the same context, the reader is assured that every good thing comes from the "Father of lights," in whom there is "no shadow of turning"—an invariability in God's nature that would seem to have moral implications).

[27]Alston, "What Euthyphro Should Have Said," p. 290.

[28]Kant, *Groundwork of the Metaphysics of Morals*, p. 414.

agreement with the moral law is a part of his nature. While we finite rational beings are possessed of inclinations that are contrary to and may become obstacles to our obedience of the moral law, God, as a perfectly rational being, suffers from no such limitation of his nature, and is thus free from all "internal obstacles" that would stand in the way of his conformity to that law. But because God *necessarily* acts in perfect accord with objective moral law, he is not *constrained* by such law.

> A perfectly good will, therefore, would be equally subject to objective laws (of the good), but it could not be conceived as constrained by them to act in accord with them, because, according to its own subjective constitution, it can be determined to act only through the conception of the good. Thus, no imperatives hold for the divine will or, more generally, for a holy will. The "ought" is here out of place, for the volition of itself is necessarily in unison with the law.[29]

To employ a familiar Kantian distinction, though God necessarily acts *in accordance with* objective moral duties, he does not act *for the sake of* or *from* duty. On Kant's view, moral obligation or duty applies only where there is some possibility of a departure from the prescribed behavior. Alston suggests that Kant is "on the right track" here.

> Where it is necessary that S will act in manner A, what sense is there in supposing that the general principle, *one ought to do A*, has any application to S? Here there is no foothold for the "ought"; there is nothing to make the ought principle true rather than or in addition to the evaluative statement plus the specification of what S will necessarily do.[30]

More generally, Alston suggests that if there is a valid conceptual distinction to be made between one's satisfying one's moral obligations and one's doing things that are morally good, "as the phenomenon of supererogation shows," then "there is no difficulty in applying the concept of moral [goodness] to an agent and his actions even if the concept of moral obligation has no application to that agent."[31] And so,

---

[29]Ibid.

[30]Alston, *Divine Nature and Human Language*, p. 263.

[31]Ibid., p. 266. I have taken the liberty of adding the word *goodness* (in brackets)

We can say that the morally good things that we are obligated to do can perfectly well have the status for God of morally good things to do, even though he is not *obliged* to do them. Justice, mercy, loving-kindness can be moral virtues for God as well as for man, though in His case without the extra dimension added to our virtues by the fact that exhibiting them involves satisfying our moral obligations.[32]

The upshot is that there is, in fact, a way of thinking of God as morally good that resists the unwelcome implications urged by Russell and others. On such a view, we may think of God's commands, which are constitutive of moral obligation for us, as issuing from God's essential goodness. The commands are thus anything but arbitrary, and God's moral authority in issuing them is grounded in the essential goodness of his character. That moral goodness, in turn, supervenes upon certain of God's essential characteristics, such as justice, mercy and love.

One likely worry at this juncture is that Alston's view suffers at the hands of the sort of dilemma—related to Euthyphro's dilemma—that Kant posed for the "theological conception" of ethics. Either we derive the concept of divine perfection from our own moral concepts or we do not. If we do not do so, then we are left only with the various nonmoral properties attributed to God. As we saw earlier, Kant thought that an appeal to such properties as justification for creaturely subservience fails to establish God's moral authority to command and pollutes one's moral motivation to obey. On the other hand, if we *do* derive the concept of divine perfection from our own concepts, then either we offer a "crudely circular explanation," or, as Kant seems to have thought, we will actually have shown that the religion-morality relationship is, in fact, the reverse of what is advocated by proponents of that theological view. Morality does not presuppose theology. Theology presupposes morality, as our theological concepts borrow liberally from our moral concepts. Does not Alston's view take out a similar loan? Else, why callest thou God *good*?

It is true that Alston appeals to such concepts as mercy, justice and lovingkindness. And it is perhaps also true that we arrive at the church

---

[32]Ibid.

with these concepts already formulated. When the preacher asserts that God is merciful, the congregation entertains the suggestion that the Creator possesses a property with which they are already familiar from their more secular commerce. Does it follow that morality is autonomous and independent of any and all theological considerations? And do we offer a "crudely circular" explanation if we suggest that such moral concepts do, in fact, "derive" from God? I think not.

There are two sorts of "derivation" here to be considered. On the one hand, God plays the role of the Good on Alston's view, and so morality derives from God in that he provides the *metaphysical* grounding for morality. On the other, our understanding of God's goodness, and of goodness in general, is *epistemically* derived from our moral concepts. We might say that, while God is metaphysically prior to morality, our moral concepts are epistemically prior to the concept of God. Or, as the medievals would have it, God is the *ratio essendi* for morality whereas morality is the *ratio cognoscendi* for our knowing God. If this view is otherwise defensible, the Kantian criticism seems to miss its target. The epistemic priority of our moral concepts does not entail that they are metaphysically prior, or, as Russell puts it, "logically anterior" to God. As I suggested earlier, it is open to the theist here to suggest that those very faculties that we employ in grasping moral concepts were designed by God himself for the very purpose of our coming to know the Good (i.e., himself).[33] Kant argued that morality cannot ultimately be derived from examples. "Even the Holy One of the gospel must be compared with our ideal of moral perfection before we can recognize Him as such."[34] But this is consistent with supposing him to be the Logos and light of the world that illumines our hearts and minds—and consciences. Perhaps, then, the very means of recognizing his perfection employs faculties forged in his own shop. If the law is "written upon the heart," would it be surprising to discover that the Author is recognized from his work?

Consider two related concerns having to do with the appropriateness

---

[33]"*Nos fecisti ad te et inquietum est cor nostrum donec requiescat in te.*" ("You have made us for yourself, and our hearts are restless until they rest in You"—Augustine's famous insight.)
[34]Kant, *Groundwork of the Metaphysics of Morals*, p. 409.

of attributing moral goodness to God. The first has been indirectly discussed in the foregoing, and so we have but to observe the implications here. We considered the objection that being told that "God does what God wills" does not seem to inform us of God's moral character. Does Alston's view face a similar objection? The question arises, In virtue of what is God said to be good? Alston's answer: "God is good by virtue of being loving, just, merciful, etc." But one may press a further question: By virtue of what are these features of God good-making features? Alston's reply: "By virtue of being features of God."[35] In a step or two we arrive at the conclusion that God is good insofar as God has the features of God. God is godly. But then Satan is satanic. We seem to have essentially the same objection that we raised against William of Ockham's version of divine command morality. In virtue of what shall we say that godly features serve as good-making features in a way that satanic features do not? The answer is that godly features serve by virtue of their *godliness*. On Alston's view, God's nature is the first principle of value, and we beg the question against his view if we insist that God and his nature must themselves be held up to some independent standard before we can meaningfully determine whether God is good. And as we have seen, any such standard faces the same difficulty, if, indeed there is anything difficult. Alston observes, "Whether we are Platonist or particularist, there will be some stopping place in the search for explanation."

> Sooner or later either a general principle or an individual paradigm is cited. Whichever it is, that is the end of the line. . . . On both views, something is taken as ultimate, behind which we cannot go, in the sense of finding some *explanation* of the fact that it is constitutive of goodness.[36]

Of course, one may ask why we should suppose that God exists as that standard. This is a good question. It is also a different question. Our present concern is whether it is coherent to suppose that he is, and to urge a model for such a theistic framework for ethics.

---

[35]Alston, *Divine Nature and Human Language*, p. 269.
[36]Ibid., p. 271.

Note too the difference between Alston's question "By virtue of what are these features of God good-making features?" and the question "By virtue of what may we *determine* whether these features of God are good-making features?" As we have seen, the answer to the latter question is that it is by virtue of our own moral faculties. Mill refused, on pain of perdition, to call any being good who lacked the sorts of good-making characteristics that he recognized among his fellow creatures. But here we are told that "God can be called good in virtue of his lovingness, justice and mercy, qualities that are moral virtues in a being subject to the moral ought."[37]

Second, some have drawn the conclusion that on any such view, God is not rightly considered to be *morally* good. One reason for supposing this stems from outright disagreement with Alston and an insistence that moral goodness is, in fact, a matter of duty fulfillment. But we are told that God *has* no duties. And so we may conclude that neither does he have *moral* goodness. Another reason is the suggestion that moral goodness requires moral agency, and such agency, in turn, requires libertarian freedom. But on Alston's view it is metaphysically impossible for God to do anything other than what is good. And so God lacks significant moral freedom and, with that, *moral* goodness. According to this objection, the term *necessary moral goodness* is oxymoronic.

Several things might be said to allay such worries. On the one hand, one might simply embrace the apparent implication. Strictly speaking, God is not literally *morally* good. Nevertheless, God necessarily acts in accordance with those principles that we recognize as morally binding for creatures such as ourselves. Here, God's goodness may be understood analogically rather than literally. Thomas Morris suggests that those principles that are *prescriptive* for us "are merely *descriptive* of the shape of the divine activity."[38]

> Although God does not literally have any duties on this construal of the duty model, we still can have well grounded expectations concerning divine conduct by knowing those moral principles which

---

[37]Alston, "What Euthyphro Should Have Said," p. 289.
[38]Thomas V. Morris, "Duty and Divine Goodness," in *Anselmian Explorations* (South Bend, Ind.: Notre Dame University Press, 1987), p. 36, italics added.

would govern the conduct of a perfect, duty bound moral agent who acted as God in fact does. We understand and anticipate God's activity by analogy with the behavior of a completely good moral agent.[39]

We may observe in a nonevaluative and merely descriptive way that God necessarily acts as God acts, and then add that the way in which he acts by necessity perfectly accords with the behavior of a perfectly good agent with moral duties. And the recognition that God's "goodness" is a matter of necessity does not negate the earlier claim that divine goodness and human goodness have a shared supervenience based in the various good-making character traits such as justice and mercy. Beyond this, some have suggested that even a necessarily good being may have a range of significant moral freedom. Are there things that it is good for God to do that are not requirements of his nature? Such acts would be the divine analog to supererogation—acts of grace—deserving of moral praise and thanksgiving. For instance, might God have refrained from creating anything at all? And it may be true, as the New Testament asserts, that it is impossible for God to lie, but might he have refrained from communicating altogether? An essentially perfect being will never violate the terms of a covenant, but the offer of the covenant itself may be an act of grace.

MORAL PARTICULARISM

I think that Alston's appeal to God's necessary goodness is promising for any view holding that morality ultimately depends on God. But as we have seen, Alston thinks the appeal to God's nature is not sufficient for grounding moral obligations.

> The divine *nature*, apart from anything God has willed or done, is sufficient to determine what counts as good, including morally good. But we are *obliged, bound, or required* to do something only on the basis of a divine command.[40]

As we have noted, we are not morally obligated to do everything that it is good for us to do. And so, Alston thinks, an additional ground

---

[39]Ibid., pp. 36-37.
[40]Alston, *Divine Nature and Human Language*, p. 273.

beyond the divine nature is needed for moral obligation. He finds this ground in divine commands. I am not persuaded by this argument. Nor do I think that is plausible to suppose that divine commands are constitutive of moral obligation.

Consider Alston's distinction between acts that are *good* for me to do as opposed to those I am *obligated* to do. It would be good for me to bake cookies and take them to my neighbors, but I am under no obligation to do so. Presumably, Alston's view implies that the status of the act would change in the event that I were to receive the command to rise up and bake. Then the act would acquire the property of *obligatoriness*, and it would be wrong of me to refrain. Perhaps this much is acceptable. But on the face of it, it appears that Alston's view implies that, while the moral *value*—good or bad—of an act may be inherent, whether it is also *obligatory* would seem to depend on whether it "should come under a divine precept," to use Ockham's language. Shall we say, then, that the property of *being obligatory* is thus "annexed"—added on—to acts? But this seems implausible once we generalize beyond select examples. Am I no more obligated to speak truth than to carry cookies when dealing with my neighbor unless there is a divine command to distinguish the "deontic status" of the two acts? Of course, *both* honesty and acts of kindness are good. But is there not a difference between the two types of act that is determined by features that are intrinsic rather than extrinsic (i.e., a relation to some divine command) to the acts themselves? Philosophers distinguish between *duties of justice* and *duties of beneficence*. The latter involve such things as extending help to those in need, while the former include the avoidance of harm, among other things. Immanuel Kant referred to duties of beneficence as "wide" and duties of justice as "narrow." The idea is that we have a standing general duty to help those in need, but we also have some degree of latitude in determining whom, when and how much we shall help. I am not obligated to donate to every charity that has gotten hold of my phone number. Despite attempts of phone solicitors to make me feel guilty, the charities probably do not have a just claim on my help, nor am I somehow wronging them or doing them an injustice if I refuse to help. But I am failing in my moral duties if I have resolved *never* to help *anyone*. I am under no obligation to carry cookies to my neighbors, but I am morally stunted if I never show kindness to anyone. Duties of justice, on the other hand, are "narrow" in that I am not afforded such latitude. All else equal, I ought to tell the truth and refrain from lying. It is not left to me to determine when or to whom or to what degree I shall be truthful.

It seems to me that the distinction between beneficence and justice runs deeper than Alston's divine command morality would allow. Even if we agree that a divine command is sufficient to render a specific act of beneficence obligatory, I cannot see why such a command is necessary in order to impose a duty of justice. Presumably, I am obligated to *refrain* from a great many things, from adultery to zoophilia. Does my obligation to keep myself to only one (human) woman obtain only because of the relation that the deeds bear to a divine command? Of course, Alston holds that acts may be either consistent or inconsistent with the divine nature, and those that are inconsistent are not good. Adultery is not good, and this is what motivates the seventh commandment. But then it is hard to see why our obligation in such cases is not simply to refrain from acts that are not good (i.e., contrary to God's nature). Why not suppose that duties of justice have their ground in the justice of God so that, command or no command, all unjust acts are immoral in virtue of this very incompatibility? What work, beyond, perhaps, an *epistemic* role, is left for the commands themselves?

Indeed, the incarnate God issued a new commandment: "That ye love one another." He added a bit by way of explanation: "As I have loved you, That ye also love one another" (Jn 13:14 KJV). That same tradition has it that *God is love*. Again, why not suppose that God's nature is the ultimate ground of the requirement rather than the command itself, as seems implied in an additional command, "Be ye holy, for I am holy"? And we may ask, is love commanded because it is obligatory for us to love one another, or is it obligatory because it is commanded? Alston's view implies the latter. But the former seems more plausible, as there seem to be deeper reasons for love, and I believe it is implied by the Christian tradition itself.

The *Imago Dei*

Christ's command to love even one's enemies is clearly not the demand that we conjure feelings of affection for, say, terrorists and tyrants. Rather, Christian charity (αγάπη) is, I believe, an attitude of unconditional regard for the worth of its object. As such, it "does not seek its own" or is not contingent upon reciprocation. It is called for regardless of the behavior of the person who is its object. As I see it, the rationale for Christ's command to love persons unconditionally is found in the unconditional *value* of such persons. Because each person enjoys a worth that is categorical in nature—independent of any extrinsic considerations—the morally appropriate attitude to take toward them is one of a categorical regard for that worth. If this much is true, then the commandment to love looks to a prior source of moral obligation, namely, the dignity of persons. If persons have dignity, then we have moral obligations that are decidedly *not* constituted by divine commands.

Here is the affirmation of an unconditional personal worth paired with an injunction to value persons accordingly. The value and the valuing are together at the very heart of a Christian ethical system. The centrality of Christian charity is seen in an exchange between Jesus and a lawyer as recorded in Luke 10:25-27 (NRSV).

> Just then a lawyer stood up to test Jesus. "Teacher," he said, "what must I do to inherit eternal life?" He said to him, "What is written in the law? What do you read there?" He answered, "You shall love the Lord your God with all your heart, and with all your soul, and with all your strength, and with all your mind; and your neighbor as yourself."

The conjunction of a love for God and neighbor is no coincidence, as the rationale for loving one's neighbor—humanity in general—is grounded in the very reasons for loving God with the entirety of one's being. And this is because the *value* of persons is, in turn, grounded in the personhood of God. Persons *qua* persons are created in the image of God in that God himself is a person. On a Judeo-Christian worldview, *human* personal dignity, though intrinsic, is derivative. The value of human persons is found in the fact that, as bearers of the *imago Dei*, they bear a significant resemblance to God in their very personhood. God and human persons share an overlap of kind membership in personhood itself, and human dignity is found precisely in membership in that kind.

I fully agree with Alston, then, that God's nature may serve as the criterion of value. But if we agree that it is sensible to say that justice, mercy and lovingkindness are good-making qualities because they are features of God, why not take a step further to suggest that *personhood* has its value also because it too is a feature of God? With this value in place, we then have a more fundamental reason for thinking that justice and mercy are virtues and a foundation for moral obligation based on what is owed to persons *qua* persons.

Alston relates a conversation with Norman Kretzmann in which Kretzmann remarked, "The really staggering fact is that the Good is a person." Precisely. Theism is committed to the view that a particular Person is both metaphysically and axiologically ultimate. This, I believe, is where a coherent theistic ethic must begin.[41]

---

[41]I thank Dave Werther for his helpful comments and suggestions.

A Naturalist Moral Realism Response

Evan Fales

WHEN PHILOSOPHERS INQUIRE about the source of moral norms, they generally are seeking an *ultimate* source: something that serves as the most fundamental ground, or truth maker, for moral truths. They are often also interested in a related question, that is, the source of human knowledge of these truths. According to Mark Linville the answers to these questions are to be found in the nature of a divine being and in the faculties we have been endowed with by that being. Linville approaches the matter by considering a classical objection to one sort of theistic ethics, namely, theories that ground right and wrong in divine commands.

The classical objection asks whether the right is right simply because God commands (or wills) it, or whether God commands or wills it because it is right.[1] If the former, then (1) there can be no (moral) justification for God's commanding or willing as he does, and (2) it is true that for any principle of action *x* whatsoever (e.g., torturing infants), God's willing/commanding it would make it morally obligatory for us to be guided by that principle. But if the latter, then the ultimate ground for moral truth is not to be found in God but exists somehow independently of his will. To this dilemma (the Euthyphro dilemma) there is a

---

[1]Divine volition theories (which ground moral principles in divine willings) have certain advantages over divine command theories; hence my equivocation here. So, for example, Linville sees the theist who accepts (1) divine commands are constitutive of moral obligation, and (2) God is good insofar as God fulfills his moral obligations as inheriting "an albatross"; (3) God is good insofar as God obeys divine commands—a consequence Alston rejects by rejecting (2). But (2) is not lightly to be rejected. Surely, if God creates sentient creatures, then God has certain moral obligations toward them. It won't do to say, as Alston (and Linville) do, that God, though unobligated, always necessarily does what is right because of his essential goodness. That ensures that God does right by his creatures, but it doesn't capture the fact that in creating sentient creatures he establishes, *inter alia*, a duty of care for them. The divine volition theorist, however, can accept (2) while not inheriting Coleridge's gooney bird. More precisely, the voluntarist should accept (1*) divine volitions (together with their "publication"—i.e., revelation) are constitutive of moral obligations, and (2*) God's goodness requires that God fulfills his moral obligations. That entails only the innocuous (3*) God's goodness requires that his actions accord with his volitions.

traditional reply, according to which the ultimate source of the Good—
the ultimate standard by which the good and the evil, the right and the
wrong, are to be judged—is to be found in God's very nature: it is either
identical with that nature[2] or is a constituent of it.

As this reply has it, that characteristic of God's nature that we call
his perfect goodness stands as the archetype, or the Form, if you will,
the standard by which all goods and evils are to be judged. The apparent strength of this solution to the Euthyphro dilemma lies in the fact
that it threads the dilemma's horns: God remains the ultimate source of
moral truth—it is not independent of him—but the moral does not
somehow depend upon the *arbitrary* will of God (and hence is not in
some ultimate way radically subjective), for the prescription is written
into God's very nature, the ultimate reality.

Drawing heavily on the work of William Alston, Linville elabo-
rates this view by articulating the relationship between the good and
the obligatory in terms of the commands of an essentially good God.
That is, there are some deeds that are not only good to do but are
supererogatory—not obligatory; these are deeds that, judged by the
divine standard, reflect or conform to God's nature in some appropriate way. And there are some deeds (and omissions) that are obligatory
because commanded by a God whose commandments are always necessarily in conformity with his essentially good nature. But, though
he agrees with Alston that a divine command is *sufficient* to generate
moral obligation, he goes beyond Alston in arguing that it is not *necessary*: thus, for example, unjust acts are proscribed and love of others
is required, whether commanded or not, because the rightness of justice and love are grounded in God's just and loving nature.[3] As Lin-

---

[2]So Aquinas—whose mystifying view is that God is entirely simple, there being no ontological
distinction between his existence and any of his essential properties—gives a version of this
response that Linville does well to steer clear of.

[3]Is a divine command to do *x* sufficient to create a moral obligation? Perhaps, if one is under an
obligation to obey God. Of course, what establishes *that* obligation can't itself, on pain of vicious
regress, be another divine command. Does the obligation to obey God trump all others? What if
God commands me to play a game of hopscotch in my driveway every morning before breakfast?
Does that put me under a moral obligation to do so? Perhaps God has some very good reason for
requiring this of me—a reason he neither tells me nor enables me to imagine. But then that reason
is what really justifies the obligation. If there really is no such reason, beyond the command itself,
then it's very far from clear to me that I have any (moral) obligation to obey.

ville puts it, "is love commanded because it is obligatory for us to love one another, or is it obligatory because it is commanded?"—and he affirms the former response.

This affirmation is telling. By Linville's lights, we are to love and be loved because our personhood is valuable, and it is valuable because it reflects the divine personhood. This prompts a question: suppose there were no divine person; *would it follow that we'd be under no obligation to respect and love one another?* Can it be that my love of others is not justified or obligatory unless their personhood images a God? That seems not only false but morally repugnant. Perhaps Linville means only to assert that both human and divine personhood are intrinsically valuable in his nature. The second claim could be (as I think) false, without detracting from the intrinsic value of human persons.

These questions are rhetorical, but they lead to an even more fundamental point. As Wes Morriston has noted, the classical response to the Euthyphro dilemma only pushes the difficulty back a step.[4] For present purposes we may put the matter as follows: Is the goodness of God good because it's part of God's nature, or is it part of God's nature because it's good? That is, if God's goodness consists in his willing and doing certain sorts of things, are those things good just because they are willed or done by God, or are they willed or done by him because they are good? To his credit, Linville recognizes the problem. Following Alston, he grasps the first horn of the dilemma:

> Godly features serve [as good-making] by virtue of their *godliness.*
> . . . God's nature is the first principle of value, and we beg the question against [Alston's] view if we insist that God and his nature must themselves be held up to some independent standard before we can meaningfully determine whether God is good. As we have seen, any such standard faces the same difficulty, if, indeed, there is anything difficult. (p. 152)

But if this response is satisfactory, why was the classic response to

---

[4]Wesley Morriston, "Must There Be a Standard of Moral Goodness Apart from God?" *Philosophia Christi,* series 2, vol. 3 (2001): 127-38.

the Euthyphro dilemma unsatisfactory? Why allow the regress to proceed for one step and then call a halt?

Now the classic response *is* unsatisfactory for the reason just noted, but Linville's own dissatisfaction with it is not well motivated. Linville thinks that a divine command theory makes the question Is God acting rightly? somehow ill-formed or meaningless or capable of only a circular or vacuous response. First, he offers an analogy: it is senseless, Linville thinks, to ask whether the platinum bar that is the standard meter is one meter long. But this, as Saul Kripke long ago pointed out, is a very far from senseless question: indeed, the International Bureau of Weights and Measures goes to *great lengths* to stabilize the length of this bar: if it were heated or stretched, it would no longer be a meter in length.[5]

Linville's second argument is that, if the right-making feature of an act is God's doing or commanding it, then the term *right* loses its meaningful content, since, if *anything* God might do or command would thereby be right, *right* does not pick out some things but not others. But that's plainly mistaken: the term would just pick out those things that God does or commands. The point here is, of course, that we have an independent grasp of the concept of rectitude, and it is a meaningful question whether the right is identical to the God-ordained.

What, then, of the argument that our appeal to a standard must stop somewhere? My reply is that there are good stopping points and poor ones. Linville's stopping point is unsatisfactory. Self-evident truths, for example, are good stopping points—perhaps as good as it gets. But there are other sorts of explanations for why the good is what it is: why, for example, love, generosity, justice and so forth are good things (for us). In my own contribution to this volume, I have tried to show how the goodness of these things follows from *our nature* (rather than from God's). That we exist and have the nature we do are contingent facts, of course. They too have explanations. But the explanation of those facts is beside the point.[6] Even if our existence and human nature were

---

[5]In fact, in part for this reason, that platinum-iridium bar is *no longer* the standard for a meter.
[6]Perhaps that explanation is not beside the point when it comes to the question of how we have gained the capacity to know moral truths. Linville suggests that the theist has a better way of

brute facts, facts with no explanation at all, it would *still* be the case that certain things are goods (for us) and that it is this that provides the ground of moral truths.

Linville's own stopping point is unsatisfactory because it simply takes our independent intuitions about right and wrong and builds them into a standard, then takes the ultimate-making feature of the standard to be its divinity. But what sort of explanation is that? What does it add to our independent knowledge of the standard or the nature of its ultimacy? Of course, as Linville rightly notes, the ontological question, the question about the ultimate ground of moral truths, is not to be confused with the question of how we may come to know those truths. But my point here is not an epistemological one but rather concerns the poverty of the theistic explanation. For even if we *know* that God is responsible for the moral law—it's being built into his nature, as it were—what makes *that* fact an explanation of its status as ultimate? Is it merely the fact that God himself is, in some sense, ultimate? But then, why not just assert that the moral law itself is an ultimate fact?

Or, to put the point a bit differently, suppose (perhaps *per impossibile)* that the Ruler and Creator of the universe were a personal being, Nec, who was essentially eternal, omnipotent, omniscient and (by *our* lights) morally corrupt. Would we then be badly mistaken about what the moral truths really are—would they, in fact, conform to an ultimate standard emblazoned upon the soul of Nec? That, I suggest, is surely an intelligible and eligible question, one that begs no question against Linville.[7]

---

explaining this, in terms of God's design of human cognitive capacities. But I find this highly doubtful, for two reasons. First, because an explanation of human cognitive faculties in terms of divine design is at least as mysterious as a naturalistic evolutionary story, and, second, because of the quite substantive work that has been done in the field of primate ethology to uncover and explain the instincts and behaviors that appear to be prototypical of human moral feelings and behaviors. As to the mysteriousness of a theistic explanation of our moral faculties, let me say just this. We understand well how the artifices of a designer can impart to an object a kind of *derived* intentionality: thus, this gadget is a can opener because that is the purpose for which it has been made, and the physical processes happening in that computer count as the computation of a sum because human programmers have assigned a certain semantics to physical states of the computer. But how could a designer confer *original* (or intrinsic) *intentionality* upon something she or he created? This is as much a mystery for the theist as it is for naturalists.

[7]It might be objected that if God is a necessary being, then Nec is an impossible being. I grant it. But then, if Nec is a necessary being, God is an impossible one. So I do not see that any question is being begged here.

A Naturalist Moral Nonrealism Response

Michael Ruse

As I read Linville's essay, it is an attempt to preserve or re-constitute some version of the divine command theory. In other words, it is an attempt to breathe life into the argument that we should do the will of God because that is in some sense what is good for us, what is our moral obligation. If only for sentimental reasons, I am sympathetic to this effort, because as a child in the years just after the Second World War I was brought up in Quakerism. Believe me, it was not easy to defend being a pacifist at such a time. Surely the war against Hitler had been a moral good? The only answer seemed to be that Jesus in the Sermon on the Mount had forbidden violence and that was an end to matters. (I am not saying that the interpretation is correct, but that that was the way we "Junior Young Friends" were taught to take it.)

But does it work? Can we answer the Euthyphro dilemma, namely, is God's will that which is good (and hence arbitrary) or is that which is good God's will (and hence presupposing some external standard), on such terms? As I read it, Linville's answer is that if we understand God's goodness as in some sense coming from God's necessary being, then we can see that God could never do or will that which is wrong, so it is okay for us to go along with what he asks of us. It is rather like God telling us to accept that $2 + 2 = 4$. In the Platonic world in which God exists, the truths of mathematics stem from his nature, from his necessity, and so he could never ask us to accept that $2 + 2 = 5$.

The obvious objection, and I think Linville is fully aware of this, is that this all seems to constrain God's will and that this is not a good thing—not a thing we expect of God, in short. A lot of Christian theology is predicated on the belief that having freedom is in itself a good thing. God could have made us all robots, but he didn't because it was better that we be free. This is the classic response to the problem of evil. It was better that Hitler have free will than otherwise, even though it led to Auschwitz. But now we seem to be saying that God is not free because God could never do anything but the good. So we are better than God, and if this isn't a reductio then it is hard to know what is.

I suspect that there might also be a secondary problem that if we make God unable to sin, then we make him more different from us and hence even harder to comprehend. The whole point about worshiping God, however, is that we must recognize his nature in some sense—otherwise worship becomes impossible. That is the point of all of the Thomistic talk about analogy. It is simply silly to say "I have absolutely no idea what God is like in any respect, but I still worship him." In any case, the whole point of the present discussion is that God's sense of goodness and our sense of goodness have to overlap significantly.

As I understand him, Linville still thinks that God has a dimension of freedom, particularly regarding whether or not to create anything in the first place. It was his choice whether there would have been a universe and humans and everything. He could—quite compatibly with his perfect and necessary being—not have created. But—and here I swing from sympathetic expositor to critic—is it the case that it is morally indifferent whether or not the universe (understood as including humankind) was created? I take it that for Richard Dawkins it is. "The universe we observe has precisely the properties we should expect if there is, at bottom, no design, no purpose, no evil and no good, nothing but blind, pitiless indifference."[1] But is this the Christian position? "And God saw every thing that he had made, and indeed, it was very good. And there was evening and there was morning, the sixth day" (Gen 1:31). It seems to me that if God necessarily does that which is good, he had no choice about the creation. Speaking for myself, I am glad it happened. But whether God was glad or not, he had to get on with the job.

There are related problems, very obvious to those of us who grew up doing philosophy of religion when Antony Flew and Alasdair MacIntyre were holding forth in a critical fashion and before they scuttled back under the comforting canvas of belief. For instance, if a being can exist that has freedom and yet always does the good, why—since we

---

[1]Richard Dawkins, *River Out of Eden: A Darwinian View of Life* (New York: Basic Books, 1995), p. 133.

humans are made in the image of God—don't we have freedom and yet always do the good? Why (and I promise after this I won't keep talking about him, or at least I will balance it with a reference to Mother Teresa) didn't Hitler go in other directions, perhaps into television with his own children's show, *Mr. Schicklgruber's Neighborhood*? (I want to go on record as saying that this wonderful image will impel me—whether freely or not—to buy hundreds and thousands of copies of this book and give them to all of my friends.)

It seems to me though that there is a deeper problem, not that I don't think that the problems I have just raised are pretty deep. Even if goodness flows from God's very necessary being, I still suspect that there is a place for some kind of extra-God justification. Take again 2 + 2 = 4. I take it that it is necessary, but under the thinking we have now it is not necessary that it be necessary. God could have made 2 + 2 = 5. And that would now be necessary. If you say that God couldn't have done other than make 2 + 2 = 4 the necessity of mathematics, then you are appealing beyond God's nature. I presume that this—that 2 + 2 = 4 is necessary but not necessarily necessary—is some version of what is known as "universal possibilism," and is often correctly ascribed to Descartes, at least the Descartes of the *Meditations*. The trouble is that it is difficult if not impossible for us to know what it would mean for 2 + 2 = 5 to be necessary. Every time we put two and three pieces of candy into a bag, there are only four? I realize that there are all sorts of strange aspects to the world where non-Euclidean geometries seem to hold and that in understanding the world we can and must use strange notions like i, the square root of minus one. But as it is, I simply cannot imagine a world—certainly a world working—where 2 + 2 = 5. In other words, it seems to me that I come back to some kind of pragmatic justification outside God. Or rather I now am saying that the kind of world God created is a world that only functions properly if 2 + 2 = 4 holds necessarily and not 2 + 2 = 5. God was involved in the creation, but once he had started working he could only do the possible. Whether God could have made an entirely different world I don't know because I am part of this one, but once he had decided on this one then he was constrained.

Now transfer the discussion over to morality. "It is good to look after the sick and poor." (Like Mother Teresa did!) This is necessary, but not necessarily necessary. God could have made it good to torture the sick and poor—dare I now say, in the manner of Hitler and his minions. But what would it mean to say that this is in some sense necessarily true (and not just an opinion or subjective truth, which I take it is the last thing that Linville wants). But again, would such a world work? Kantian sorts of issues start to come in here, and even if we don't get logical contradictions a case can be made for saying that we get social contradictions. A world where anything goes—no love, no trust, no sense of obligation—simply doesn't function. (I don't have to rely just on Kant. As a Darwinian evolutionist, I believe this.) Perhaps, as I said about mathematics, God could create a world where Hitler is the saint and Mother Teresa the devil, but it isn't this one. Once God started creating this world, he was constrained. He could do no other.

So I am not sure that Linville has dug himself and his God out of the hole that Euthyphro (or rather Plato) so carefully dug to trap us. But if a nonbeliever might presume to stretch a friendly hand across to a believer—because as I said at the beginning, I do have a sentimental attraction to the divine command theory—surely what I have been arguing in the past few paragraphs gets us halfway at least to Aquinas's solution, namely, natural law theory. First there is eternal law: "This rational guidance of created things on the part of God . . . we can call the Eternal law." Then we humans fit into this. "This participation in the Eternal law by rational creatures is called Natural law."[2] The point is that God does not just decide things capriciously. Human morality has to fit with human nature, and this means with what is natural, with what is the proper functioning of our being, physical and mental. Morality is God's will, but it isn't arbitrary. Being unkind to small children is immoral because in some sense it is unnatural to us as human beings. Perhaps God could have made another world, but given the kind of world that he did make, morality like mathematics was part of the package deal.

One final word. By being so helpful (!) at this point, am I not under-

---

[2]Thomas Aquinas, *Summa Theologica* (London: Burns, Oates & Washbourne, 1952), I.1a2ae, q. 91, art. 1.

mining my own naturalistic take on ethics? Not really. I go into the exercise with God not existing—I don't have faith, and I see all of the problems both theological (how can someone's death two thousand years ago help me by proxy?) and philosophical (how do you explain Auschwitz?). So frankly for me this is all a bit like a board game—fun but not ultimately serious. At another level it is serious, because these are serious issues whether you are a believer or not—like doing non-Euclidean geometry before Einstein found a use for it—and because (and this is very important to me) I think we can see room for a comfortable relationship between believers and nonbelievers. As a Darwinian, as a naturalist, I am very welcoming of natural law theory, with its roots in an Aristotelian connection between that which is natural and that which is good. I too think that food and sex and love and caring are good things. I don't want to go the further step to God, but if someone does, I can criticize theologically and philosophically, but not in my role as a Darwinian. And that, it seems to me, is a happy accommodation for both believers and nonbelievers.

A Moral Essentialism Response

Keith E. Yandell

> Why not suppose that God's nature is the ultimate ground of the requirement [to love one another] rather than the command. . . .
>
> God and human persons share an overlap of kind membership in personhood itself, and human dignity is found precisely in membership in that kind.—Mark Linville (pp. 156, 158)

Professor Linville begins with Russell's restatement of the Euthyphro dilemma: either God makes something good by choosing that it be so (making morality arbitrary) or God commands what is, independent of God, already good (thus compromising divine sovereignty). The gist of Alston's reply, partially accepted by Linville, is simple: God is inherently good and God's commands are determined by God's goodness. So morality is not arbitrary and God remains sovereign. In order to provide context for considering Linville's view, we will note three relevant senses in which the claim "Necessarily, God is good" can be understood. Only the third is Linville's. The others look at alternative ways of responding to Euthyphro and clarify Linville's view by contrast with it.

"GOD" AS A TITLE

The claim that "Necessarily, God is good" is central to Linville's view. First, two readings that Linville does not take. One is that "God" is a title and that goodness is a necessary condition for deserving it. "Necessarily, if x holds the title 'God' then x is good." This sense is used by Paul Moser in *The Elusive God:* "Along with many other people, I use the term 'God' as a supreme *title* that connotes an authoritatively and morally perfect being inherently worthy of worship."[1]

This is neutral concerning whether "God exists" is a necessary truth. Interestingly, Moser adds, "If God would be praiseworthy for being perfectly authoritative, as seems plausible, then we should allow that

---

[1]Paul Moser, *The Elusive God* (Cambridge: Cambridge University Press, 2008), p. 32.

God *could* fail the test, even if God doesn't actually fail it."[2]

One way to develop this idea is this: suppose there are necessary moral truths which constitute the basic principles of morality. These truths are propositions that exist "on their own"—they cannot be caused. Then it is not possible for God to cause them. Possibly true notions of divine sovereignty do not require that God can do what is in principle impossible. Thus God's nonarbitrary commands accord with these principles and God's sovereignty is uncompromised.

The idea expressed in the second Moser quotation *suggests* (it is not developed) that the proper view is not that *God has goodness as an essential property* but that *God has moral perfection in virtue of God's choices and actions* (e.g., those involved in the internal life of the Trinity, as well as those in relation to the creation). If so, it is best seen as ascribing libertarian freedom to God so that God's goodness is a product of God's choosing rightly.

This view need not worry its proponents as to whether God may change character over time. Assume that God exists everlastingly (in time) rather than timelessly. Then if God is omniscient, and this includes knowledge of God's future, if ever God chooses wrongly at time T then God knows at every time T^* before T that God will do so. But then God knows at T^* that God intends to choose wrongly at T, and so is not morally perfect at T^*. The upshot is that if God is ever morally imperfect, then God is always morally imperfect, and if God is ever morally perfect, then God always is.

VOLUNTARISM

A second sense is given by voluntarism. To illustrate this view, Linville quotes from Ockham and Scotus. The idea is that God arbitrarily establishes by fiat what goodness shall be—there being no rational basis for any such choice. There are deep problems with the view. First, on one natural reading, voluntarism ascribes to God libertarian freedom without criteria for choice. Baby-stomping (Linville's example) might have been obligatory, and just happens not to be. It seems generally, and groundlessly, supposed that once God has made up God's mind, it will

---

[2]Ibid., p. 67.

not change. On voluntarism, whether change of divine mind would be wrong was decided arbitrarily (if at all). So perhaps tomorrow one will be obligated to put on one's boots.

Second, a central feature of this view is the denial that any character, action or state of affairs is intrinsically good or bad. Such properties are *annexed* by arbitrary divine fiat. On this understanding the most that can be made of "God is good" is something like "God has arbitrarily annexed to God the property 'being good'" with "being good" having a content arbitrarily supplied by God. This is not what Christian theism means by God being good. Or again, it is possible on this view that God has deemed it good that all the content of revelation is false, and that those who accept it are damned. For these reasons, and others, the view has not been widely accepted.

ALSTON-LINVILLE

A third sense is provided by the view that goodness is a property which God necessarily has. Metaphysical goodness includes at least omnipotence, omniscience and causal independence. Moral goodness is goodness of character, manifested in always rightly acting, and Alston includes moral perfection in metaphysical. The question remains as to the source of obligation.

We are not obligated to do something just because doing it is good or creates something good—there are too many good things to be done. Doing some good things is incompatible with doing others, and some things that would be good to do are supererogatory. On Alston's view, only if a perfectly good Creator commands that something be done is one obligated to do it. So now, it is claimed, we have a nonarbitrary divine command theory. On this view, goodness is basic to rightness: if nothing were good, nothing would be right either. Absent divine commands, there would be no obligations, though for Alston these commands are not arbitrary.

Here Linville disagrees with Alston on the grounds that on Alston's view once again rightness becomes an annexed property. God will not want wrong things to be done, but as Linville notes, this does not entail that it is *only* God's will or command that makes them wrong. This raises an important question: if we have an obligation not to act wrongly, whose source is independent of God's commands, what is its source? Necessary truths that connect goodness and rightness? If so, what exactly is the status of those necessary truths? Thoughts necessarily in the mind of a necessarily existing God or abstract objects? One advantage of moral essentialism is its ability to explain this.

To develop Linville's departure from Alston, suppose God created persons but gave them no commands. People would still have intrinsic worth. Why wouldn't they have rights? If they had rights, why wouldn't they have obligations to one another? For that matter, why wouldn't a good God be obligated not to harm them for pleasure? Why wouldn't it be wrong for God to do so? It seems that, given that there are persons, and even absent divine commands, there would be obligations. It also seems that both God and created persons have them. None of this is so on Alston's view. This view can include that God has duties to God: if it would demean God to do A, it would be wrong of God to do A, and God has a duty to God not to do A. If so, then God can have duties and moral laws, and thus God can be a moral agent.

From one perspective, on moral particularism, strictly speaking God is not a moral agent. One reason for denying moral agency to God is that God cannot do anything that is not good. This view too has its varieties. On one understanding, there is always a best for God to do, and it is impossible for God not to do it. Necessarily, God does the best thing. On a second understanding, there can be equally good things at the top of the list of things that God can do, and God can choose among them. On a third understanding, there are good things that God can do that are optional, and God may or may not act in a supererogatory manner. On the first understanding, God has no libertarian freedom. On the second, God does seem to have libertarian freedom that can never be used in a worse way than choosing something at the top of the list. On the third, God seems to have libertarian freedom among things God, as perfectly good, need not do at all.

FREEDOM

Linville claims that "Necessarily, God is good." Thus God has no libertarian freedom regarding God's goodness. It is worth spelling out the consequences of taking this view. On one widely held view of God, God is morally good by nature and had no choice about the matter. On a less widely held view, God is a moral agent whose perfect goodness is chosen by God. There are relevant conflicting views of freedom here. They are important for their own sake and for filling out a Linville-type view. One is compatibilism, for which it is not necessary to be free in any way that requires for responsibility that one, under the actual circumstance of choice, could do anything other than what one does. If one claims that God has necessary existence in the Alston-Linville sense, and embraces the view that God can only act when there is a best way to act and cannot but act in the best way, then there is no possibility that God does not do just as God does. It is impossible that God do *A* and yet not have done *A*, and it is impossible that God did not do *A* and yet could have done *A*. God is "free" in the sense that God is not caused to do what God does "from outside" and could do otherwise only in the sense that, had it not been necessarily true that God did what God did and did not do what God did not, God could have done otherwise. Compare: had it not been a necessary truth that 17 is prime, 17 might not have been prime. This sense of "could do otherwise" expresses no logical possibility.

Replace the view that God can only act when there is a best way to act with the view that God can act when two or more ways of acting rank even in goodness. Then, where the tied actions are *A* and *A**, there are possible worlds in which God does *A* and possible worlds in which God does *A**. Then God can have more than freedom "from outside determination" in that it is compatible with God's nature that God do either of two things with no better reason to do one than the other. This will make a very limited libertarian freedom available to God. If we replace this view by, or add to it, the third view regarding supererogation, then there is more scope for divine libertarian freedom.

The basic issue regarding libertarian freedom is whether God could in principle act wrongly. To be clear: the issue is not whether God has left the straight and narrow path of moral perfection. The question concerns what moral perfection *is*. The different views can be spun off an analogy. Consider the Mona Lisa, and assume it to be aesthetically perfect. Then it deserves as high a degree of aesthetic praise as can be offered. But it is not responsible for its beauty—it possesses a beauty that was entirely given to it. Its beauty is praiseworthy, but not it for having it—it does not get credit for producing its beauty. Now suppose we have a person Mary who always makes the right choices for the right reasons and always carries them through in the right way. Suppose also that determinism is true—either logical fatalism for which every truth is a necessary truth and every falsehood a necessary falsehood, or every event, choice and action is caused in such a fashion that, given the past and the laws of nature, it could not have failed to have occurred exactly as it did. Then it seems that Mary is not responsible for her goodness. Her goodness is praiseworthy, but not her for having it. If this is moral praise at all, it is analogous to the aesthetic praise just described.

Now we can state the issue. For a *compatibilist* concerning freedom— one for whom the truth of determinism is perfectly compatible with moral responsibility—Mary is a moral saint. Her right choices and actions are produced by a causal chain that predates her but goes through her mental states out into her behavior. Thus she did contribute to her choices and action, though her doing so was as it had to be. She even could have done otherwise in a sense that the compatibilist trumpets as sufficient for responsibility: *had circumstances been different, she could have done otherwise.* For logical fatalism it would have been logically impossible that they have been otherwise. For a plain determinist it would have required a change in the past or in the laws of nature for them to have been otherwise. None of necessary truths, the past or the laws of nature are under Mary's control. Still, Mary is free in whatever sense responsibility requires.

For a *libertarian* concerning freedom, Mary in a determinist world is a product of factors beyond her control. What is logically impossible, what is past and what the laws of nature are, are beyond her, and what they determine, she "chooses" and "does." She is a conscious automaton. What is crucial for her being a moral agent is that, on occasions when her choice or action has moral significance, *she could have done otherwise in the situation in which she actually was.* A libertarian concerning freedom with full courage of her convictions will view God as a moral agent whose moral perfection is due to God's use of God's freedom. The issue of what constitutes divine freedom is central to our view of the nature of God.

CONCLUSION

This response has discussed Linville's view in contrast to two other distinct views (Moser's and voluntarism), and one view with which it only partially differs (Alston's). Setting voluntarism aside for reasons noted, this leaves us with three strong responses to Russell-Euthyphro questions. Linville shows that these questions do not imply that God is irrelevant to morality, but (so far as I can see) the question as to what grounds obligations remains unanswered in his essay.

Alston holds that God is the paradigm of the good, and God's commands are constitutive of obligation. Were there no command against torture for pleasure, would it be wrong to torture for pleasure? The answer is yes; thus (even if there is such a command) the wrongness here is not due to divine command. Linville agrees, adding that while God is the paradigm of the good, obligations are based on the intrinsic worth of persons, human and divine. But this is incomplete: it *assumes* that persons having intrinsic value entails that we are obligated to respect them. If this is so, then there are propositions that are necessary truths of some such form as "If X is a person, then X ought to be respected." Such propositions are either thoughts necessarily had by a necessarily existing God or they are abstract objects. This returns us to moral essentialism.

Contributors

Evan Fales is Associate Professor of Philosophy at the University of Iowa. Fales's extensive publications in the philosophy of religion, epistemology and metaphysics include *Causation and Universals* (Routledge, 1990), *A Defense of the Given* (Rowman and Littlefield, 1996) and *Divine Intervention: Metaphysical and Epistemological Puzzles* (Routledge, 2009).

Mark Linville teaches philosophy at Clayton State University. In addition to numerous articles and book chapters, including "The Moral Argument" in *The Blackwell Companion to Natural Theology* (Wiley-Blackwell, 2009), Linville is the coeditor (with David Werther) of *Philosophy and the Christian Worldview* (Continuum, 2012) and is the coauthor (with Paul Copan) of *The Moral Argument* (Continuum, forthcoming).

R. Keith Loftin is Assistant Professor of Humanities at The College at Southwestern. He holds an M.A. in humanities (University of Dallas), an M.A. in philosophy (Louisiana State University), and is a doctoral candidate at the University of Aberdeen.

Michael Ruse is the Lucycle T. Werkmeister Professor of Philosophy at Florida State University, where he also directs the Program in History and Philosophy of Science. An ardent proponent of Darwinian naturalism, Ruse has published numerous books and articles, including *Taking Darwin Seriously* (Prometheus Books, 1998) and *Biology and the Foundation of Ethics* (coedited with Jane Maienschein, Cambridge University Press, 1999).

Keith Yandell is the Julius R. Weinberg Professor of Philosophy at the University of Wisconsin-Madison. He has written *Hume's "Inexplicable Mystery": His Views on Religion* (Allyn and Bacon, 1971), *The Epistemology of Religious Experience* (Cambridge University Press, 1993) and *Philosophy of Religion* (Routledge, 1999), as well as numerous papers on God and morality.

Index

From IVP Academic